The Best
of
SLAVIC COOKING

The Best
of
SLAVIC COOKING

Alojzije Kapetanović and Ružica Kapetanović

Published by Associated Book Publishers, Inc.
P.O. Box 5657, Scottsdale, Arizona 85261

LC Card No. 81-71605

ISBN:0-910164-06-1

PRINTED IN THE UNITED STATES OF AMERICA

TABLE OF CONTENTS

INTRODUCTION

INTRODUCTION

The Slavs are an Indo-European people who share a common history and heritage, as well as many traditions and eating habits. Specific foods have become well known throughout the world by their methods of preparation and by the festivities and holidays with which they are associated.

The Slavs migrated from the East to an area running from the Baltic Sea in the North of Europe, to the Adriatic Sea in the West, and to the Black Sea in the south. This migration has left a strong cultural imprint in Eastern Europe. These people created such powerful medieval empires as the Russian Empire, the Great Moravian Empire, the Polish Empire and the Great Croatian Empire. Today, Slavic people inhabit the lands of Russia, Croatia, the Ukraine, Bulgaria, Czechoslovakia, Poland and Slovenia. Each nation has seen intermarriage with other nationalities and races, and the introduction of outside influences from neighboring lands. As a result, the Slavs share a common ancestry and heritage, but have developed independent contemporary histories, cultures and traditions.

Many foods and culinary traditions are linked to religious feasts and festivities. Various religious faiths can be found in the countries inhabited by the Slavs, but the majority of Slavs are Christian. In the countries of Poland and Czechoslovakia and in Slovenia and Croatia the major religion is Roman Catholicism, while in Russia, Bulgaria and the Ukraine the majority of the people adhere to Orthodox Christianity. In Croatia, the legacy of the Turkish occupation in the 14th century has left a substantial Moslem population.

3

The lands that the Slavs settled and developed were blessed with fertile soil on which a variety of grains and vegetables flourished. There were fields for planting and grazing; forests full of game and lakes; and rivers and seas that overflowed with seafood. Because of the common heritage of the Slavs, we find many similarities in the foods of all the Slavic peoples. While certain other dishes are variations of a theme adapted to the national or provincial tastes, each nationality has its own distinct national preparations.

A formal Slavic meal typically begins with the serving of *Zakouski*, which are *hors d'oevres*. The *zakouski* range in variety from cheeses and meat specialties, to stuffed eggs and caviar.

Caviar is the most famous Russian pre-meal specialty and there are numerous varieties. Black and red caviar are two of the types that might be served. The black variety of caviar is from the sturgeon, while red caviar is obtained from salmon and has larger grains. Caviar is served cold with hot toast and lemon juice or lemon wedges. It may also be accompanied by *blini*, small buckwheat pancakes.

The Croatians frequently serve an appetizer called *Burek* which consists of spiced ground beef rolled in paper-thin filo-type dough and baked to a golden crust. The *burek* is served cut into bite-sized pieces.

Other *zakouski* dishes served by the Slavs include meat *patés*, cold meats, salamis and smoked salmon. *Zakouski* are traditionally served with vodka in Russia, *šljivovica* in Croatia and Slovenia, *raki* in Bulgaria, and other spirits toasting the health of family, guests and friends.

Although appetizers are usually reserved for guests, the main meal of the day generally begins with a serving of soup. The variety is endless from basic clear chicken and beef soups and cold summer soups to thick hearty soup stews which can serve as a complete meal when served with whole wheat bread or hearty Russian Black Bread.

On cold Russian days, soup provides warm nourishment. Russians are also fond of cold soup dishes that are eaten with light summer lunches. A thick soup called *Schi* is made from cabbage and smoked meats. Sour *schi* is a variant of the basic soup with a tart flavor derived from the addition of sauerkraut. *Borsch* is another popular soup that originated in the Ukraine and has a base made from beets. This rich, thick soup is almost a complete meal. *Borsch* is a beet soup which can be served hot or cold and is prepared with a variety of vegetables. Meat can be added for extra flavoring. It is usually served with sour cream. There are many variations on the basic recipe. We have included a Ukrainian version of hot *Borsch*, a Russian version of Cold *Borsch* and a Polish derivative called *Barszcz* which is flavored with mushrooms.

Solyankas are soups that are made with meat or fish and assorted vegetables. *Sol* in Russian means salt and the name *solyanka* comes from the taste given to the soup by the addition of salty pickled cucumbers. The soups are garnished with sour cream or flavored with dill or parsley, and they are served with slices of fresh bread, *piroshki* or hard-cooked eggs.

Another hearty soup that is prepared in the Ukraine is Hunter's Giblet Soup, a rich soup-stew made with chicken giblets, and a variety of root vegetables. Hunter's Giblet Soup can fortify anyone with a sincere appetite.

The Czechs and Slovaks are also fond of steaming bowls of soup filled with dumplings. Included in this volume are three favorites—Potato Soup, Oxtail Soup and Caraway Soup. If any flavoring can be associated with the Czechoslovakian kitchen then it is the caraway seed. This seed is used not only in soups and with sauces, but can also be found in vegetables, poultry, meat, and in baking.

Many Slavic people are fond of cold soups in the summer. Bulgarian *Tarator,* perhaps the most famous of these soups, is made with yoghurt, walnuts and cucumbers. In addition to cold Borsch, we have included two other popular cold soups—Polish Cold Cherry Soup and Cold Apple Soup. Try these excellent cold summer soups very well chilled and be sure to serve them over ice cubes.

Fish provides an important element in Slavic cooking. The rivers, lakes and seas that are found in and around Eastern Europe are sources of a great variety of seafood. Seafood is plentiful in Poland both from fresh water, such as rivers and lakes, and from the Baltic Sea. Large quantities of carp, trout, pike, salmon, cod, eel and herring are consumed by the Poles. Fish is also eaten in great quantities by the Bulgarians and the Ukrainians. The Black Sea and freshwater rivers such as the Dneiper and the Danube provide Ukrainia and Bulgaria with an abundance of seafood. The Adriatic Sea is the greatest source of Croatia's fish and shellfish. The Adriatic provides hundreds of types of seafood, including such delicacies as red mullet, Adriatic prawns, lobsters, oysters, tuna, shrimp and countless other shellfish.

Perhaps the most popular fish prepared in Slavic countries is the versatile carp. Carp is a soft-finned fish that is reared in artificial ponds. The flesh of the fish is firm and tasty. It is usually purchased live, brought home and held in fresh water for several hours until cooking time. Then it is dressed and prepared according to tradition. Carp is a traditional dish served on holidays, especially on Christmas Eve, in both Catholic and Orthodox countries.

In Slovenia, an entree of carp may be a spicy Paprika Carp or it may be a jellied carp mold. Bulgarians are fond of carp stewed with walnuts and then baked in the oven. In Czechoslovakia, carp is prepared by dousing the skin of the fish with hot vinegar to turn the skin dark. It is then boiled and served as Christmas Carp. Croatians prepare Champagne Carp by simmering the fish in champagne with mushrooms.

Herring from the Baltic Sea may be prepared in a marinade of spices which is allowed to sit for a few days. It may also be fried or boiled and served with horseradish sauce. Eel in Wine is a Polish delicacy prepared by cooking eels and mushrooms in white wine. Byeluga Sturgeon or White Sturgeon is found in the Black Sea and is the source of the famous Byeluga Caviar. Sturgeon may grow to over four feet in length and has an excellent flavor when cooked.

Freshwater fish, such as sturgeon and salmon play an important role in the diet of Russia. In addition, saltwater fish such as cod, mackerel and sole are marketed and eaten throughout Russia. Salmon is prepared with horseradish and sour cream sauce, grilled with olive oil or boiled, flaked and baked in a pastry dough called *kulebiaka*.

With their location on the Adriatic Sea, the consumption of seafood is very important to the Croatian coastal provinces of Dalmatia and Istria. Dalmatians boast that the sea provides them with a different type of seafood for every day of the year. The region is proud of many distinctive dishes, including Dalmatian Brodet, an excellent fish stew made from saltwater fish fillets in a light tomato sauce base.

Poultry has always been plentiful in the Slavic countries. The home grown birds are not cooped up, but are generally allowed to run freely in the yards of the villages. This allows for the breeding of fowl of the finest quality.

Chicken, turkey, duck, goose, partridge, quail, capon and grouse are all very popular. Poultry is prepared in countless ways from roasting and frying to well-seasoned stews and casseroles. Poultry is often prepared with dumplings. It may also be baked or sauted in a sour cream sauce, a method of preparation that is used in all the Slavic countries. Included in this collection is an excellent Chicken in Sour Cream dish from the Ukraine.

Goose and chicken dishes frequently find their way to festive holiday tables. It is after the beautiful capital city of the Ukraine that the classic preparation, Chicken Kiev, is named. Chicken Kiev is a dish of chicken breasts with a filling of mushrooms and melted butter. The melted butter is sealed within the meat and serves to baste the tender chicken while cooking.

In Croatia turkey is prepared as *Podvarka* roasted on a bed of sauerkraut. This keeps the bird moist and enhances it with a wonderful tangy flavor. In Poland turkey is stuffed with Polish sausage and breadcrumbs before roasting.

Roast goose is a favorite holiday dish everywhere. The Czechs and Slovaks frequently serve goose roasted with caraway seeds during the Christmas holiday season. Roast squab and roast capon stuffed with chestnuts also add to variety to their choice of poultry dishes.

The wide range of popular meat dishes utilize either veal, pork, lamb or beef. Meat is served in casseroles, stews, skewered or roasted whole.

The Slavs have a tradition of raising domesticated pigs and preparing pork dishes. The people of the Mediterranean regions and the Moslem populations had always viewed pork as unsuitable for consumption. In those areas it is sheepherding that traditionally provided meat and fat. Pork continues to be very popular in most areas and distinct variations in its preparation may include Jellied Pork's Feet or Fried Pork Chops. In addition to a large variety of methods of preparing fresh pork, the Slavic people have created numerous forms of *charcuterie* and these delicacies may be found hanging in meat shops from Poland to Bulgaria. *Kielbasa* sausage in Poland may be called *kobasica* in

Croatia, but it is still as enticing to eat. Sausages may be spiced with red or black pepper, paprika, garlic, marjoram or with any one of a number of other spices. Their flavor may be mild and salty or it may be piquant and spicy hot. Canned and smoked hams are also produced in Slavic countries where in most rural homes the attic is used to smoke and cure hams and bacon. In many Slavic countries no Christmas is complete without Roast Suckling Pig.

Bigos, the Polish national dish can be prepared in many ways. History tells us that it was originally prepared with game as the main ingredient. Today, pork is substituted. Our version of the famous the hunter's stew is prepared by flavoring the pork with sauerkraut, Polish sausage and mushrooms and then baking the stew in the oven.

Ghivetch, a Bulgarian vegetable casserole is also prepared in Croatia where pork is added and it is known as *Djuvedje.* We have included a Bulgarian version of meatless Ghivetch and a Croatian version of Djuvedje with pork.

Ukrainians prepare pork with sauerkraut or *Lokshnya* with Ham. *Lokshnya* are noodles that are prepared at home with butter and sour cream. They may be served with a red cabbage salad or with a beet salad with tomatoes.

Beef, although prepared by Slavic people, is not as popular as it is in the United Sates and Canada. It is not raised as readily because of the lack of adequate grazing land for cattle. Russian Beef *Kotlety* are small meat patties made from ground beef. The preparation of the meat patties requires that the meat be soaked in milk which leaves the *kotlety* juicy and tender after cooking. Another elegant meat dish that comes from Russia is Beef Stroganoff named after the Tsarist family. This dish is made from tender beef strips cooked in a tart sour cream sauce.

In Czechoslovakia beef is prepared as *Svičkova,* a beef

roast served with a spicy sweet and sour cream sauce. Another popular beef dish from Czechoslovakia requires that beef ribs be braised and then sauted with kohlrabi.

Veal has a greater popularity than does beef because it is easier to raise and is considered a tastier type of meat. Veal, pork and lamb are used in stews and soups, or as meat patties and kebobs, which are grilled over hot coals. Veal cutlets that are dipped in egg, and then breaded and fried, have become famous as a dish of the Austro-Hungarian Empire. They are a favorite delicacy of the Slavic people of Easten Europe.

A popular Ukrainian veal dish is roast veal breast served with potatoes that have been cooked with the meat in the meat's juices. Bulgarians simmer veal with prunes for an interesting variation. Polish veal patties are sauted in sour cream and served with Cauliflower à *la Polanaise,* or with a potato salad. Veal is also prepared as a Hunting Pie, spiced, sauted in wine and then baked in a flaky pastry dough.

Zagreb, the capital of Croatia, is a city with a refined taste for food. Veal is eaten throughout Northern Croatia and Zagreb Veal Cutlets are a delectable creation prepared by stuffing tender slices of veal with thin strips of Dalmatian *prsut* ham and Trappiste cheese. The stuffed cutlets are then breaded and fried in butter. This dish is usually served with a fresh green salad and a tasty dressing.

Lamb is especially popular in the southern Slavic countries. Bulgarians are especially fond of lamb and mutton and certainly no Moslem festive occasion is complete without lamb roast on a spit. Bulgarian Roast Lamb is prepared by basting with olive oil and wine vinegar while the meat is roasting. In the northern Slavic countries mutton is frequently stewed with vegetables or sauerkraut. One of the most popular methods of preparing lamb is to grill the meat on skewers. The lamb is cut into cubes, soaked in a spicy marinade, then placed on a skewer to be grilled over open coals. Grilled meats continue to be popular in those countries that were occupied by Turkey. In Croatia, this dish is known as *ražnjići,* in southern Russia it is known as shashlik. Try substituting other meats for the lamb or combining several. The meat can also be alternated on the skewer with chunks of vegetables, mushrooms, pineapple, pickles or apples.

Dairy cattle are an important part of food production. The rich milk and cream is used to make butter and an endless variety of cheeses. In the mountainous regions, cow's milk is replaced by goat's milk and new varieties of cheese are found there. Each country produces numerous types of cheeses. Some types of cheese can be found everywhere, while other distinct types are found only in certain regions of a country. The butter and cream that is available on farms goes into all types of cooking and baking. In most Slavic cuisines, soups, stews and casseroles are garnished with fresh or sour cream.

Casseroles may serve as an introduction to a meal or they may be the main course of the meal. A casserole dish that often serves as an appetizer to a feast but can also serve as a separate meal is Stuffed Cabbage Rolls. This specialty is made in many countries of Eastern Europe. It can be prepared with fresh cabbage leaves in a tomatoe sauce or with pickled cabbage leaves. Ukrainian rolls of fresh cabbage leaves are stuffed with ground meat and rice and cooked in meat stock. The tender rolls are named *golubtzi,* which in Ukrainian means "little doves." Croatians use pickled cabbage to prepare *sarma*—lovely cabbage rolls filled with ground beef or veal, bits of smoked ham and rice. The rolls are cooked in a tangy sauerkraut sauce giving a distinct flavor to what can be considered the Croatian national dish.

The fertile land settled by the Slavs is now productive farmland which yields a bounty of fruits and vegetables. Meats are often combined with the abundant vegetables to create unique stews and casseroles.

Almost any vegetable can be stuffed with a combination of rice, meat or cheese, but stuffed peppers seem to have universal popularity. The peppers are cored and stuffed with rice or with a meat and rice mixture. They are usually baked in the oven but can also be slowly simmered in a rich tomato and green pepper sauce.

The type of vegetable produced in each country is dependent upon the climate and terrain of that country. In the colder northern climates of Poland, Russia and Czechoslovakia, cabbage, beets and root vegetables are widely grown. Other vegetables have a limited season. Cabbage which can be eaten fresh or pickled and used to make thick soups, is eaten by all Slavs; but it can be considered a national dish of Poland. It is served in salads or with meats, in stews, in soups or stuffed with meat or a meat and rice mixture.

Croatia, Slovenia, Bulgaria and the Ukraine have longer growing seasons and warmer temperatures. In addition to root vegetables, they raise tomatoes, eggplant, peppers and cucumbers—ingredients that go into the making of the famous Bulgarian salad, *Shopska Salata*. The Bulgarians have evolved as agricultural experts and therefore their cuisine reflects this in its use of vegetables, grains and fruits. Legumes such as peas, beans and lentils are eaten readily, while grains such as rice, barley, corn and wheat also add to the diet. Dried white beans are the most popular and are known as the national dish of Bulgaria. Bulgarian Bean Soup is a hearty specialty.

Other vegetables such as leeks, onions, tomatoes, eggplant, spinach, okra, carrots and cabbage are also bountiful in the warmer areas and are prepared both as vegetables and as ingredients in casseroles. The Ukrainians grow considerable corn and are very fond of eating roasted ears of corn, as is done in the United States.

The pickling of vegetables is carried on by many Slavic households. It was a method of preserving vegetables over the winter months and today green tomatoes, peppers, sauerkraut, mushrooms and pickles are still preserved in this manner.

The Slavs enjoy dill and horseradish as flavorings. Cloves and garlic are also used profusely in their cuisines. For flavoring, the Czechs enjoy caraway seeds and marjoram as well as fresh dill, cloves and garlic. The versatile cooking of Poland also incorporates the use of capers and horseradish. Bulgarians, Croatians and Slovenians are especially fond of flavoring their foods with spices and herbs such as paprika, red pepper, minced garlic, onion juice, and cumin.

Mushrooms are found all over the forests of the Slavic lands and are eaten in a variety of ways. Mushrooms are used as a side dish, pickled for use in winter, and used as a garnish for soups and meats.

The Slavic meal usually ends with a variety of fresh fruits, but for special occasions elaborate desserts may be in store. Orchards of apples, pears, peaches and plums provide fruit that is eaten fresh or used in preserves and jams. Fruit is also used to make fruit salads, stewed fruit and desserts such as Baked Apples, Cherry *Savijača*, Apricot and Peach Sauce and Strawberries Romanoff.

The variety of desserts in Russia runs from elegant preparations such as Strawberries Romanoff and *Charlottka* to simple *Cranberry Kissel,* with many fine creations in between such as *Khvorost* cookies, traditional Easter fare called *Pashka* and delicate tea cookies.

Strawberries Romanoff is a luscious dessert of strawberries that have been marinated in orange juice and curacao and are served with whipped cream. This tempting speciality is named after the Russian dynasty—the Romanoffs.

Peter the Great, who became the Czar of the Empire in the 17th century, brought many foreign dishes to the Russian court. During his reign peasant cooking at the court gave way to refinement and a classical Russian cuisine. French chefs cooked for the royalty at court and Peter's reputation as a *gourmand* became reknowned. French cuisine and the stately and refined presentation of food came to a zenith with Catherine the Great. Her obsession with the French and their culture required lavish meals to become the standard at royal gatherings. Czar Alexander I carried on the French tradition in the Russian kitchen and a chef in his employ named Antoine Careme, is credited with creating the marvelous dessert called *Charlottka*, also known as *Charlotte Russe*. *Charlottka* is made by lining a mold with lady fingers and filling it with custard or Bavarian cream and decorating with whipped cream and strawberries or candied cherries. Today, the meaning of the word *charlotte* has been extended and it is used to refer to any type of cold molded dessert made with lady fingers, sponge cake, cookies or even bread.

In the Ukraine dessert preparations range from simple Milk *Kissel* to more elegant dishes, such as Filled Baked Apples in which the apples are stuffed with almonds, raisins and rum. Poppy seeds are used in baking and in desserts. Poppy Seed Cakes and Poppy Seed Loaves are Ukrainian specialties.

Making dessert pancakes developed into an art in the Austro-Hungarian Empire and in France. These thin pancakes have come to be known as *crêpes* in French, *palacinke* in Croatian, *palacinky* to the Czechs and Slovaks, *palacsinta* in Hungary and *Palatschinken* to the Austrians. Each nation will vehemently defend this delicary as its own, although its origin is not known. The variety of fillings is limited only by the chef's imagination. We have presented a basic Croatian version of *palačinke* with walnut cream filling and cottage cheese filling. For a change, try them with cherry pie filling, any type of jam, grated chocolate or ground walnuts with brown sugar.

The dessert choices to be found in Poland are varied. They often include fruits or pastries. Especially noteworthy are Polish Cinnamon Pears topped with whipped cream, a delicious *Babka* or a Fruit *Mazurek.* Beekeeping and the use of honey are longstanding traditions in Poland. Honey is used profusely in baking cakes, tortes, cookies and other sweet delicacies. Sweet jams are made from berries, plums, apricots, pears, cherries and apples. These jams are then used as fillings for desserts, pastries and cakes.

Desserts for the Bulgarians are not as often rich cream pastries as they are puddings made from rice, fresh fruit salads spiked with wine and brandy, nut and Middle-Eastern nut pastries with layers and layers of crisp paper-thin dough drenched in honey or syrup.

Early in Slavic history barley and wheat became the primary grains of their diet. Wheat and rye, which are grown on farms today, go into the making of breads, rolls, buns and other baked goods, forming the basis of the Slavic diet. The wheat grown in Slavic countries is of a high quality and baking has been turned into a sophisticated art. In addition to breads and rolls, fresh ingredients such as butter, milk, cream and eggs are used to create exquisite tortes, cakes and pastries.

The hard-working Slavic people needed basic solid food and became hearty bread-eaters. Even today, hardly a meal goes by that some type of bread is not eaten in the Slavic home. This may be a delicate crusty white bread fresh from the oven, heavy whole wheat bread, rye bread with caraway seeds, hot corn bread or the famous Russian Black Bread. In the past, homes had clay ovens in the yard that were used for the baking of bread. Long flat paddles were used to place the bread in the oven and remove it when it was baked. Today, in most of the smaller cities and towns, the baker bakes fresh bread early in the morning, when it can be purchased warm from the oven.

In Poland, breads, rolls and other baked goods are consumed readily. Breadcrumbs are sprinkled on meats, vegetables and poultry, and this style of garnishing food has come to be known as *a la Polonaise*. The best known Polish pastries are the *Babka* and the reknowned *Rum Baba*. Legend has it that Stanislaus Lezinski, King of Poland during the 17th century, invented the pastry and gave it the name of his favorite storybook hero—Ali Baba. Later the name was changed to *Rum Baba*. Whatever its origin this is a delightful dessert and quite simple to prepare.

The Czechs and Slovaks enjoy yeast buns filled with fruit jams, especially prune jam. They also make rich tortes filled with nuts, eggs and cream. Meringues are popular throughout Czechoslovakia and many varieties fill pastry shop windows.

Nuts are used in all types of baking in the Slavic countries and many have national favorites using nuts as the main ingredient. *Potica* is a rich walnut roll which every Slovenian cook is accomplished at baking.

Tortes are baked throughout Eastern Europe. The main difference between cakes and tortes is one of richness. Although they are made from basically the same ingredients, tortes tend to be richer and more elaborate because they rely on nuts, chocolate, butter, eggs and whipped cream. Unfortunately, tortes will not keep very well. They generally must be used fresh. Despite this, they are certainly rewarding to bake, especially for guests and special occasions. We have included a sample of several varieties. Experiment decorating them in different ways with walnuts, hazelnuts or almond slices, grated chocolate, whipped cream and candied cherries.

The Croatian coast is dotted with groves of trees that provide figs, pomegranates, almonds, lemons, oranges and the famous Croatian sour cherries known throughout the world as Dalmatian *maraschino* cherries. This is only a sample of the fruits that abound and are used in preparing elaborate desserts and pastries.

The most distinctive Croatian pastries are the delicate flaky *savijaće*. The light, crisp, flaky dough used to make Middle Eastern desserts of many layered, nut-filled pastries drenched in syrup and honey was adapted by Croatians who rolled it around a filling of sweetened apples, cherries, poppy seeds, nuts, cheese and even cabbage. The rich glutenous flour produced in the Bačka region of Croatia has helped Croatian bakers to develop the art of making this incomparable pastry to high perfection, stretching the pastry dough to semi-transparency. The delicate pastry was quickly adopted in the rest of the Austro-Hungarian empire where the delicacy became known as *strudel* in German and *retesek* in Hungarian. Although it requires some time and application to learn the technique, once it is mastered, making the *savijaća* pastry becomes surprisingly simple. The results are certainly worth the effort.

The Slavic peoples of Croatia, Slovenia, Russia, Poland,the Ukraine, Czechoslovakia and Bulgaria have developed independent national cuisines and culinary traditions, which have become an integral part of the culture of each nation. Various external influences have come to play on each Slavic group and its cooking so that the cuisine of each nationality is diverse, yet still they all share the basic Slavic foundation of cooking that was brought to these lands in the past. Over the centuries, the Slavic cook has developed a sophisticated art of cooking and baking which has come to require a high degree of skill. These cooking techniques have been passed on from family to family in each succeeding generation. Even today, cooks in these countries generally do not refer to a cookbook but retain hundreds of recipes mentally. Through practice, they have acquired the knack for blending the correct quantities and combinations of ingredients, spices and flavorings to prepare each dish.

The Slavs are fond of fine food prepared with care and have an appreciation of high quality ingredients. It is this fondness that has inspired this cookbook, *The Best of Slavic Cooking.* All the recipes and unique methods of food preparation that are found in each Slavic country could not be included here but it is hoped that what has been included is representative of the best of Slavic cooking.

HORS D'OEUVRES

HORS D'OEUVRES

*

BUREK
(Croatia)

Meat Filling:

1 c. chopped onion	1½ c. beef stock
3 tbsp. shortening	1 tbsp. chopped parsley
1 lb. ground beef	1 tsp. ground red paprika
½ lb. ground lamb	1 egg, lightly beaten
¼ c. butter	¼ c. flour
	salt and pepper to taste

Saute the onion in the hot shortening until it becomes a golden brown. Add the ground meat and cook for about five minutes, stirring constantly. Drain the meat if it has released much fat. Add the salt, pepper, paprika or red pepper, parsley and egg to the mixture. Stir well over the heat for a minute or two. Melt the butter in another saucepan. Add the flour, a little at a time, stirring after each addition. When browned, add the beef stock and simmer until thickened. Add the sauce to the meat mixture. Place in the refrigerator for about an hour.

Dough Ingredients:

4 c. dry cake flour	1 tbsp. vinegar
1 tsp. salt	2 tbsp. oil
1 egg	1¼ c. warm water, approx.

21

Sift the flour with the salt into a large mixing bowl twice. Make a well in the center. Drop in the egg, vinegar and oil and mix ingredients well. Add one cup warm water. Work all the ingredients into a firm dough. Add more water as required to make a smooth and elastic dough. Continue to knead the dough until it is soft and begins to blister. Experience will help you decide when the dough is soft enough. The dough must be very soft, but smooth enough not to stick to the hands. Divide the dough into two balls. Grease a deep bowl with butter or margarine. Place the balls of dough in the bowl. Turn them around so that they will be greased on all sides. Cover the bowl with a damp kitchen towel and allow it to rest in a warm place for approximately half an hour. Spread a large table with a tablecloth. Dust generously with flour. Roll the dough very thin with a rolling pin. Brush with a little warm oil. Begin stretching the dough by pulling from the center out with floured fists. Pull the dough in all directions. When the dough covers more than half the table and the center is very thin, begin pulling the edges with the fingertips. Walk around the table always pulling from the center. Be sure to pull the dough evenly from all sides. When the dough is fully stretched, it should cover the whole table and should be thin enough to read newsprint through it. Allow the dough to drape over the edges of the table. Trim the edges with kitchen shears or tear the thick edges away gently. Allow the dough to dry for 10-15 minutes. Grease the dough generously with melted butter or with oil, then spread with the meat filling. Gently lift the tablecloth at one end of the table, pulling so that the dough will roll as the tablecloth is pulled upward and toward you. Brush the top of the burek with a little melted butter. Bake in a hot oven at 400° until the burek is golden and crisp. Cut into sections and serve hot. Burek also makes an excellent entree for a light lunch. Serves 6.

*

*

EGGPLANT "CAVIAR"
(Russia)

1 eggplant
1 onion, finely chopped
½ c. olive oil

1 hard-cooked egg
juice of half a lemon
salt and pepper to taste

Wash the eggplant and bake in the oven at 350° for one hour or until soft. When the eggplant has cooled, remove the skin and finely chop the meat. Add the onion, chopped egg, lemon juice and olive oil. Season with salt and pepper and then mix well. Serve chilled with toast.

*

BRAIN "CAVIAR"
(Bulgaria)

1 lb. calf's brain
2 c. boiling water
½ c. olive oil
2 hard-boiled eggs, sliced

2 tbsp. chopped garlic
juice of half a lemon
¼ c. olives, chopped
1 tbsp. parsley, chopped
salt and pepper to taste

Wash the brain in cold water. Clean the brain and remove all veins and skin. Place in boiling water and allow to cook for 20 minutes. Drain the water and pass the brain through a sieve. Add the oil, parsley, garlic, lemon juice and olives. Mix well and season with salt and pepper. Place the "caviar" on a serving dish and garnish with egg slices. Serves 4.

*

CHOPPED GOOSE LIVERS
(Croatia)

3 goose livers, chopped	3 tbsp. white wine
5 tbsp. butter	¼ c. sour cream
2 tbsp. chopped onion	1 c. mushrooms, sliced
	salt and pepper to taste

Heat the butter. Saute the onion in the butter for 3-4 minutes, stirring constantly to prevent sticking. Add the thinly sliced mushrooms and the goose livers. Season with salt and pepper. Add the wine, a tablespoon at a time, stirring after each addition. Simmer until the goose livers are tender. Remove from heat. Stir in the sour cream. Serve on crackers or very thin slices of toast.

*

CHICKEN AND LIVER PASHTET
(Russia)

½ lb. chicken livers	½ lb. bacon
½ c. olive oil	3 eggs, well beaten

1 c. sour cream
1 c. flour
4 tbsp. butter, melted
1 c. grated cheese
salt and pepper to taste
2 apples

½ c. chicken stock
1 c. cooked chicken
½ lb. mushrooms
¼ c. breadcrumbs
½ c. chopped ham
2 tbsp. lemon juice

Combine the lemon juice and olive oil. Finely chop the cooked chicken, the chicken livers, apples, bacon, and mushrooms. Mix well and set aside. Mix together the chicken stock, beaten eggs and the melted butter. Combine the chicken meat, mushrooms, apples and ham. Season with salt and pepper to taste. Add the beaten eggs, flour and chicken stock to the chicken meat mixture. Grease a baking dish and layer the bottom of the dish with the sour cream. Add half the grated cheese. Place a layer of the chicken meat mixture in the dish, then a layer of the chicken liver mixture. When the mixtures are placed in the baking dish, top with the remaining cheese and then with the bread crumbs. Bake in a moderate oven for half an hour. Serve hot with bread slices.

*

CHOPPED HERRING
(Poland)

1 c. pickled herring, cubed
1 onion
4 hard-cooked eggs
1 c. sour cream

2 tbsp. dill
1 tbsp. chopped parsley
¼ tsp. paprika
salt and pepper to taste

Finely chop the onion, eggs and dill. Combine the herring, onion and eggs. Add the parsley, dill and paprika. Season with salt and pepper. Stir in the sour cream and blend well. Serve with whole wheat or rye bread.

*

PIROSHKI
(Russia)

1 c. flour, sifted	¼ lb. ground beef
4 tbsp. butter	3 tbsp. sour cream
3 tbsp. chopped onion	1 tbsp. minced parsley
1 hard-cooked egg	salt and pepper to taste

To prepare meat filling, sauté the onion in a little oil, add the ground beef and brown. Season the meat with salt, pepper and parsley. Allow to cool and mix in the chopped egg. Season the flour with a little salt and cut in the butter to form small crumbled balls of dough. Add the sour cream and mix well to form a uniform ball of dough. Place the dough in the refrigerator to harden. Remove the dough when ready and roll out onto a floured board. Cut dough into 4-inch squares. Place into the center of these squares spoonfuls of the meat filling and fold over and seal the edges together by moistening with water and then pinching together. Place the piroshki in the refrigerator again and allow dough to harden. Bake the piroshki for half an hour at 350°. Serve warm.

*

*

CHEESE SPREAD
(Czechoslovakia)

1 c. cottage cheese
¼ c. butter
½ onion, finely chopped
1 tbsp. anchovies
1 tsp. mustard

1 tsp. paprika
2 tbsp. sour cream
1 tsp. caraway seeds
1 tsp. capers

Mash the cottage cheese and anchovies and mix well. Add the remaining ingredients and blend well. Chill in the refrigerator for several hours and serve on dark bread.

*

RUSSIAN MEATBALLS
(Russia)

½ lb. ground beef
2 slices bread
1 egg yolk

1 egg, beaten
¼ c. breadcrumbs
3 tbsp. flour
salt and pepper to taste

Soak the bread in a little milk. Combine the beef and egg yolk and season with salt and pepper. Drain the bread and mix with the meat. Wet the hands and mold small meat balls and roll in flour, beaten egg and then in the breadcrumbs to form a crust. Heat enough butter in a skillet to deep fry the meat balls until golden brown.

*

CHICK-PEA AND SESAME SEED SPREAD
(The Ukraine)

½ c. chick peas
3 tbsp. sesame seed
1 tbsp. lemon juice

1 clove of garlic, minced
1 tbsp. water
2 tbsp. olive oil
salt and pepper to taste

Soak the chick peas overnight and cook over low heat for 2 to 3 hours until soft. Mash the sesame seeds and mix with the garlic, water, lemon juice and olive oil. Mix well. Mash the chick peas and add to the sesame seed mixture. Season with salt and pepper and blend well. Serve on toasted black bread.

*

CHICKEN LIVER SPREAD
(Poland)

¼ lb. chicken livers
½ c. of milk
2 hard-cooked eggs
1 onion

1 c. ham, finely chopped
2 tbsp. butter
3 tbsp. oil
salt and pepper to taste

Finely chop the ham, eggs and onion. Soak the chicken livers in the milk for 2 to 3 hours. Drain the livers and finely chop. Heat the butter in a skillet and saute the onion in it.

Add the livers and fry until golden brown. Mix the livers with the eggs, ham and oil. Season with salt and pepper and blend well. Spread on crackers or toast.

*

COTTAGE CHEESE SPREAD
(The Ukraine)

¼ lb. cottage cheese   1 clove of garlic, minced
2 tbsp. sour cream   ½ tsp. paprika
1 tsp. worcestershire sauce   salt to taste

Combine the cottage cheese and the garlic. Add the sour cream, paprika and worcestershire sauce. Season with salt and mix well. Serve on crackers with a garnish or serve as a dip.

*

BLACK OLIVE PASTE
(Bulgaria)

1 c. black olives, pitted   1 tbsp. anchovy fillets
2 tbsp. chopped onion   4 tbsp. olive oil
                         1 tbsp. lemon juice

*Chop the olives and mash them into a fine paste. Mash the
anchovy fillets and add them to the olive paste, along with
the onion. Stir in the olive oil and lemon juice and mix well.
Serve on crackers or toast.*

*

RUSSIAN EGGS
(Russia)

8 hard-cooked eggs   1 c. sour cream
½ c. caviar   juice of ½ a lemon
2 tbsp. chopped chives   1 tbsp. chopped parsley
                                  pepper to taste

*Slice the eggs in half lengthwise, and place on individual
dishes. Combine the caviar, sour cream, lemon juice, chives
and parsley. Season with pepper and mix well. Spoon the
caviar and sour cream mixture over half an egg. Place in the
refrigerator to chill before serving. Serve with crackers.
Serves 6-8.*

*

*

ANCHOVY PASTE
(Poland)

12 anchovies
¼ c. sour cream

3 slices bread
¼ c. milk
2 tbsp. lemon juice

Cube the bread and soak it in the milk. Mash the anchovies and combine with the sour cream and lemon juice. Drain the bread and add to the anchovy mixture. Stir into a smooth paste. Serve on crackers.

*

EGGPLANT AND PEPPER SPREAD
(Bulgaria)

1 eggplant, cubed
1 green pepper, finely diced
1 red pepper, finely diced
1 chili pepper, finely diced
2 tomatoes, chopped
1 onion, chopped

¼ c. olive oil
4 cloves of garlic, minced
3 tbsp. lemon juice
4 tbsp. chopped parsley
salt and pepper to taste

Heat the olive oil in a saucepan. Brown the onion in the olive oil. Add the tomatoes and peppers and saute until tender. Add the eggplant and garlic and continue to saute until the eggplant is tender. Mash the eggplant well and add the onion, the peppers, and the tomatoes. Stir in the parsley and lemon juice. Season with salt and pepper and mix well. Chill the spread for several hours. Serve with bread, toast or crackers. Serves 6.

*

STUFFED TOMATOES
(Czechoslovakia)

6 tomatoes	2 cloves of garlic, minced
½ c. cooked ham, diced	4 tbsp. chopped parsley
½ c. sausage, diced	3 tbsp. butter
2 onions, finely chopped	¼ tsp. paprika
	salt and pepper to taste

Wash the tomatoes and slice off the tops. Remove the pulp. Melt the butter in a saucepan and saute the onions, garlic and tomato pulp for 15 minutes. Add the ham, sausage, parsley and paprika. Season with salt and pepper. Cook for an additional 10 minutes, stirring to prevent sticking. Stuff the tomatoes with the meat mixture. Butter a baking dish and place the tomatoes in the dish. Bake in a moderate oven at 350° for 30-45 minutes. Serve warm. Serves 6.

*

*

ĆEVAPČIĆI
(Croatia)

1 lb. ground beef
1 lb. ground lamb
2 tbsp. lard or shortening
2 onions, finely chopped
2 cloves garlic, minced

2 tbsp. flour
1 tbsp. parsley
1 egg, lightly beaten
1 tsp. paprika
salt and pepper to taste

Heat the lard in a medium saucepan. When the foam subsides, add the onions and garlic and cook them for a few minutes until the onions are slightly browned. Transfer the onions to a deep bowl. Add the meat, egg, flour, salt, pepper, parsley and paprika. Mix well. When all the ingredients are well combined, shape little sausages from the mixture about 2 inches long and arrange them on a plate. Cover the plate and refrigerate the ćevapčići for at least two hours before cooking. Ćevapčići are most frequently barbecued on an open charcoal grill. Grill them for about 15-20 minutes. They should be a dark brown on the outside and very well done on the inside. Turn them over frequently while grilling. If preferred, they can be cooked in a saucepan in a little hot oil or lard. They must be turned often so that they do not stick. Serve sprinkled with chopped onions or with an onion salad. Serves 6-8.

SOUPS
AND
SOUP ADDITIVES

SOUPS AND SOUP ADDITIVES

*

CARAWAY SOUP
(Czechoslovakia)

1 tsp. caraway seeds
6 c. meat stock or water
4 tbsp. flour

4 tbsp. butter
salt to taste

Heat the butter and add the flour. Allow the flour to brown and to form a roux. Place the stock or water in a pot and add the roux. Season the soup with salt and add the caraway seeds. Cook for half an hour. Add soup noodles and cook a few more minutes. Serves 5-6.

*

GREEN BEAN SOUP
(Croatia)

6 c. water
1 lb. green beans
2 tbsp. butter
1 tbsp. flour

½ tsp. minced garlic
½ c. sour cream
1 tbsp. chopped parsley
salt and pepper to taste

Chop the green beans and cook them in salted water until tender. Heat the butter or shortening over low heat. Increase the heat and brown the flour and garlic in it. Add the flour and garlic to the green beans. Season with salt, pepper and chopped parsley. Continue cooking for another half hour. Add the sour cream just before serving. Serve with bread sticks. Serves 6.

*

STAJERSKA SOUR SOUP
(Slovenia)

3 lbs. pig's knuckles	1 tbsp. chopped garlic
¼ c. fat	6 c. water
1 carrot, sliced	½ tsp. paprika
1 onion, finely chopped	1 tsp. parsley
¼ c. chopped celery	½ c. vinegar
1 lb. potatoes	4 tbsp. flour
	salt and pepper to taste

Peel and cube the potatoes. Clean and wash the pig's knuckles. Split the knuckles and place in a pot with the carrot, onion and celery. Pour in the water and allow to cook for 45 minutes. Add the potatoes 15 minutes later and allow to cook for half an hour. Heat the fat in a saucepan and add the flour, garlic, parsley and paprika. Allow to fry until the flour browns. Add the roux to the soup and bring the soup to a boil. Add the vinegar and season with salt and pepper. Serves 6.

*

*

KIDNEY SOUP
(Poland)

1 lb. beef kidneys, sliced
6 c. boiling water
2 onions, finely chopped
¼ c. celery root, diced
¼ tsp. caraway seeds
croutons

4 tbsp. butter
4 tbsp. flour
¼ c. carrots, sliced
¼ c. parsnip, diced
dash of paprika
salt and pepper to taste

Heat the butter in a saucepan and saute the kidneys, onions, and caraway seeds. Season with paprika. Add the flour and allow to brown. Place the water in a pot and add to it the kidneys, carrots, parsnips and celery root. Season with salt and pepper. Allow the soup to cook for half an hour. Serve with the croutons. Serves 5-6.

*

RASSOLNIK
(Russia)

1 lb. beef kidney
¼ c. pickles, sliced
2 tbsp. dill-pickle juice
1 tbsp. chopped parsley
2 c. sorrel, finely chopped
¼ c. sour cream

6 c. water
1 onion, finely diced
4 potatoes
2 tbsp. oil
¼ c. celery, diced
salt and pepper to taste

Peel and slice the potatoes. Remove any gristle and membrane from the kidney. Wash and cut the kidney into large pieces. Place in a saucepan, cover with cold water and allow to cook for about an hour and a half. Heat the oil, add the onion, carrot and celery and saute. Add the pickle slices, potatoes and the stock that the kidney cooked in. Cook for another 30 minutes. Season with salt and pepper. Fifteen minutes later, chop the kidney pieces into smaller pieces and add to the soup along with the sorrel and the pickle juice. Bring to a boil again. When ready to serve, garnish with sour cream. Serves 6.

*

HUNTER'S GIBLET SOUP
(The Ukraine)

6 c. water	2 bay leaves
2 c. chicken or turkey giblets	1 leek, sliced
	1 tbsp. parsley
4 potatoes	¾ c. millet
1 carrot, sliced	1 onion, finely chopped
¾ c. bacon, diced	salt and pepper to taste

Peel and cube the potatoes. Wash and chop the giblets. Place in the water to cook. Season with salt and pepper. Cook the giblets for one hour and then strain the stock. Fry the bacon in a saucepan to render the fat. Add the vegetables and saute for 10 minutes. Add the vegetables, giblets, bay leaves, millet and parsley to the stock. Cook the soup until the vegetables are tender. Serves 6.

*

*

OXTAIL SOUP
(Czechoslovakia)

1 lb. oxtails	1 tbsp. butter
6 c. water	3 tbsp. mushrooms, sliced
2 tbsp. carrots	2 tbsp. parsnips
1 onion, finely chopped	1 tbsp. chopped parsley
2 tbsp. celery, diced	salt and pepper to taste

Place the water in a pot, cut up the oxtails and add to the water. Cook the oxtails for 2 to 2 1/2 hours. Melt the butter and add the onion, carrots, mushrooms, parsnips and celery when the butter is heated. Saute the vegetables for 5 to 10 minutes. Strain the soup and clean the bones. Return the meat to the soup and add the vegetables. Season with salt and pepper. Add the parsley. Allow the soup to cook for another 15 to 20 minutes. Serves 6.

*

BORSHCH
(The Ukraine)

1 lb. beef, cubed	3 c. shredded cabbage
1 lb. pork, cubed	7 c. water
1 tbsp. flour	1 potato, cubed
¼ c. white beans, cooked	1 tbsp. wine vinegar
1 bay leaf	3 peppercorns

3 beets, cut into strips
1 tomato, chopped
¼ c. smoked bacon
½ tsp. sugar
2 c. sour cream

1 carrot, sliced
1 small onion, chopped
2 tbsp. butter
½ tsp. parsley, minced
salt and pepper to taste

Heat the butter in a saucepan and brown the beef, bacon and pork. Add the meat to the water and season with peppercorns and bay leaf. Allow the meat to simmer until tender. Cool the soup and skim off the cold grease. Warm the soup and add beets, potato, carrot, tomato and onion. Season with salt and sugar. Cook the soup for about half an hour. Add the cabbage and cooked beans. Slowly stir in the flour, parsley and then the wine vinegar. Cook the soup for another half an hour. Serve with the sour cream on the side. Serves 6.

*

COLD BORSHCH
(Russia)

1 lb. beets, cut into strips
1 onion, finely chopped
¼ c. beet greens, chopped
¼ c. chopped green onions
1 c. sour cream

4 c. beef or chicken stocks
1 c. tomato sauce
1 cucumber
salt and pepper to taste

Place the beets in the meat stock and cook until tender. Place the finely chopped onion and beet roots in water and cook for 5 minutes. Add the onions, beet greens and tomato sauce to the beets. Season with salt and pepper and allow to cook for 2-3 minutes, mixing well. Allow the soup to cool completely before serving. Finely chop the cucumbers and green onions. Combine the cucumbers, green onions and sour cream and serve with the cold borsch. Serves 4.

*

SHCHI, CABBAGE SOUP
(Russia)

1 lb. beef, cubed	1 soup bone
6 c. water	1 onion, finely chopped
2 tbsp. butter	3 peppercorns
2 tbsp. flour	1 bay leaf
1 carrot, sliced	½ head cabbage, shredded
1 tsp. parsley	1 tsp. dill
1 c. sour cream	salt to taste
1 c. buckwheat groats	

Place the beef, soup bone, peppercorns and bay leaf in the water and cook for two hours. Allow to cool and skim, remove the bone. Melt the butter in a saucepan and saute the carrots and onions until tender. Sprinkle the vegetables with the flour and saute an additional minute. Add the carrot and onion to the soup. In another pot heat three cups of water and season with half a teaspoon salt. Bring to a boil and add the buckwheat, stirring constantly. Turn down the heat, cover the pot and simmer for 40 minutes. Add the shredded cabbage to the soup and cook for another half an hour. Season with salt to taste. Five minutes before the soup is ready add the parsley and dill. Before serving, stir in the sour cream. Serve with the buckwheat kasha. Serves 6.

*

CHESTNUT SOUP
(Poland)

1½ lb. chestnuts	2 egg yolks
6 c. vegetable stock	2 tbsp. butter
1 slice of bread, cubed	salt to taste

Make a cut in each of the chestnuts and place them in boiling water for 15 minutes. Drain the water. Remove the outer shell of the chestnuts. Immerse them in boiling water and remove the inner skin. Heat the butter in a saucepan and saute the chestnuts until tender. When the chestnuts are ready, mash them and combine with the egg yolks. Season the mixture with salt. Heat the vegetable stock and stir in the chestnut mixture. Allow the soup to cook for 10 minutes. Melt some butter in a skillet and allow it to get hot. Add the bread cubes and fry quickly to make croutons. Add the croutons to the soup and serve immediately. Serves 6.

*

CALF'S BRAIN SOUP
(Poland)

1½ lbs. calf's brains	4 tbsp. butter
6 c. beef stock	3 eggs, well beaten
½ c. celery, chopped	2 carrots, sliced
1 tsp. parsley	3 tbsp. flour
	salt and pepper to taste

Heat half the butter in a saucepan and saute the calf's brains in the hot butter for 5 minutes. Mash the brains and add in the flour. Heat the remaining butter in another pan and fry the celery and carrots until tender. Combine the brains and the vegetables and pass through a sieve. Add to the beef stock and season with salt and pepper. Allow the soup to simmer for 5 to 10 minutes. Season with parsley. Just before serving, slowly add the beaten eggs, stirring constantly. Serves 6.

*

SHAV
(Russia)

6 c. beef stock
4 eggs, well beaten

1 lb. chopped spinach
salt and pepper to taste

Heat the beef stock. Add the fresh spinach and allow to cook for 5 minutes. Season the soup with salt and pepper. Add the beaten eggs slowly, stirring constantly. Allow the soup to cook an additional minute or two. Serve with sour cream. Serves 6.

*

*

BEAN SOUP
(Bulgaria)

1 lb. navy beans	4 onions, finely chopped
6 c. beef stock	1 tbsp. vinegar
1 tsp. parsley, chopped	½ tsp. dill, chopped
dash of paprika	salt and pepper to taste

Wash the beans and add to the beef stock. Season with salt and pepper. Add the onions and cook the soup until the beans are tender. Add the vinegar, dill and parsley, and simmer for another five minutes. Sprinkle the soup with paprika and serve immediately. Serves 6.

*

MOCK KASHA SOUP
(Croatia)

6 c. clear beef stock	2 tbsp. lard or shortening
2 eggs	2 tbsp. flour
½ c. water	½ tbsp. parsley
	salt to taste

Beat the eggs well and add the water to them. Season with salt. Melt the shortening and add the flour to it. When the roux begins to brown, pour in the egg mixture and cook 5-6 minutes, stirring constantly. Add the beef stock and parsley to the mixture. Stir and cook for another 10-15 minutes. Garnish with noodles or dumplings. Serves 6.

*

LAMB SOUP
(Bulgaria)

1 lb. lamb, cubed	3 onions, finely chopped
6 c. water	½ c. rice
1 tbsp. flour	½ tsp. mint
½ c. olive oil	salt and pepper to taste
2 c. yoghurt	

Heat the olive oil in a saucepan and brown the meat. Add the onion and rice and saute for another 5 to 10 minutes. Season with the mint and fry another minute or two. Add the meat, onions and rice to the water and season with salt and pepper. Thicken the soup with the flour by adding it slowly, stirring to avoid lumps. Cook the soup for an hour or until the rice is tender. Serve the soup with the yogurt. Serves 6.

*

*

ASPARAGUS SOUP
(Poland)

6 c. vegetable stock
1 lb. asparagus, cooked
  and mashed
1 c. cream

2 tbsp. butter
2 tbsp. flour
4 eggs, well beaten
salt and pepper to taste

Heat the butter in a saucepan and add in the flour. Allow the flour to brown to make a roux. Add this roux to the vegetable stock, along with the asparagus. Bring to a boil and cook for about fifteen minutes. Season the soup with salt and pepper. Combine the sour cream and eggs and mix well. Pour this mixture into the soup and allow to simmer for another five minutes. Serves 6.

*

BARLEY SOUP
(Slovenia)

½ c. barley
6 c. beef or chicken stock
½ c. celery, finely chopped

1 onion, finely chopped
1 carrot, sliced
1 green pepper, chopped
1 tsp. salt

Heat 4 cups of water, add the salt and the barley. Cook the barley for approximately two hours or until the water has evaporated. Heat the meat stock, add the barley, onion, carrot, green pepper and celery and allow the soup to cook for an additional half an hour. Serves 6.

*

SOUR SHCHI, SAUERKRAUT SOUP
(Russia)

1 lb. sauerkraut	1 tbsp. tomato puree
6 c. beef stock	1 bay leaf
3 peppercorns	2 tbsp. flour
1 onion, finely chopped	2 tbsp. butter
1 carrot, sliced	2 c. sour cream
	salt to taste

Heat the butter in a saucepan and saute the onion and carrot. Add the flour and tomato puree. Wash and drain the sauerkraut and add to the onion and carrot. Simmer the sauerkraut for half an hour. Add the sauerkraut, onion and carrot to the beef stock. Add the peppercorns, salt and bay leaf. Allow the soup to cook for another hour and a half and serve with sour cream. Serves 6.

*

*

MUSHROOM SOUP
(The Ukraine)

¾ c. mushrooms, sliced	1 onion, finely chopped
4 c. water	2 tbsp. barley
3 tbsp. butter	2 potatoes
2 c. milk	½ c. sour cream
	salt and pepper to taste

Peel and cube the potatoes. Heat the butter in a saucepan and saute the onion and mushrooms for 5-10 minutes. Place the barley in the water and season with salt and pepper. Cook the barley for 40 minutes. Add the potatoes and cook for another 15 minutes or until the barley is soft. Pour in the milk and cook for five more minutes. Just before serving stir in the sour cream. Serves 6.

*

DALMATIAN SOUP
(Croatia)

6 c. beef stock	3 tbsp. flour
¼ lb. cooked macaroni	2 tbsp. chopped onion
¼ c. butter	½ c. Parmesan cheese

Heat the butter over low heat. Increase the heat and brown the onion in the hot butter. Add the flour and make a golden roux. Add this roux to the beef stock. Stir well. Allow to cook for 20-25 minutes. Add the cooked macaroni and grated cheese before serving. Serves 6.

*

BEEF SOUP
(Bulgaria)

7 c. beef stock	3 tbsp. rice
1 lb. ground beef	4 eggs, well beaten
1 onion, chopped	¼ c. sour cream
1 tbsp. parsley, finely chopped	1 bay leaf, chopped
	salt and pepper to taste

Heat the stock and add in the rice. Remove the rice when cooked and combine with beef, half the eggs, parsley and onion. Season with salt and pepper. Roll the meat into small balls and add to the beef stock. Add the bay leaf. Allow the soup to cook over low heat for twenty minutes. Add the remaining beaten eggs slowly to the soup, stirring constantly. Allow to cook for one minute. Stir in the sour cream and serve immediately. Serves 6.

*

*

BARSZCZ
(Poland)

6 beets, pared and cubed   rye bread crusts
warm water   2½ tbsp. sugar

Place the beets in a jar and cover with warm water. Add in the sugar and breadcrumbs. Cover the jar with a cloth and place in a warm spot for 6-8 days. This produces a kwas which is the foundation of the soup.

6 c. meat stock   ½ c. mushrooms
5 beets, pared and diced   3 cloves garlic, crushed
                             salt and pepper to taste

Add the beets, mushrooms and garlic to the meat stock. Season with salt and pepper. Allow the soup to cook for one hour. Stir in the kwas and mix well. Bring to a boil and cook for another five minutes. Serve with boiled potatoes or dumplings. Serves 6.

*

STURGEON SOLYANKA
(Russia)

6 c. water   2 lb. whole sturgeon
1½ c. tomato pulp   ½ c. black olives, chopped

1 c. pickles, diced
1 cucumber, peeled and
  diced
1 tbsp. capers
1 tbsp. lemon juice

2 onions, finely chopped
1 bay leaf
1 tbsp. chopped parsley
1 tbsp. dill
2 tbsp. butter
salt and pepper to taste

Clean and fillet the fish. Place the head and bones in the water. Add the parsley, dill, capers and bay leaf. Season with salt and pepper. Cook for 45 minutes over low heat. Remove the fish head and bones. Dice the fish fillets. Heat the butter in a saucepan. Add the onion, tomato pulp and fish. Cook for 5 minutes. Add this to the soup along with the pickles, lemon juice cucumbers and olives. Season with salt and pepper once again. Allow the soup to cook for another fifteen minutes. Serve garnished with lemon slices. Serves 6.

*

POTATO SOUP
(Czechoslovakia)

6 c. water
1 onion, finely chopped
1 c. celery, diced
1 carrot, sliced
1 parsnip, cubed
2 tbsp. flour

6 potatoes
1 tbsp. chopped parsley
1 tbsp. dill, finely chopped
¼ tsp. marjoram
3 tbsp. butter
½ c. mushrooms, sliced
salt and pepper to taste

Peel and cube the potatoes. Heat the water and add the potatoes, onion, parsnip, celery, carrot, parsley, marjoram

---

and dill. Season with salt and pepper. Allow the soup to cook for half an hour to 45 minutes until the potatoes are tender. Heat the butter in a saucepan, add the mushrooms and saute for 5-10 minutes. Add the flour and allow to brown. Add this roux to the soup and allow to cook for another ten minutes. Serves 6.

*

SPINACH SOUP
(Croatia)

1½ c. chopped spinach	6 c. beef stock
1 onion, finely chopped	½ c. Parmesan cheese
1 tbsp. butter	¼ c. smoked bacon, diced
2 tbsp. flour	salt and pepper to taste

Saute the spinach and onion in the butter for about fifteen minutes. Season with salt and pepper. Fry the bacon in its own fat. Add the flour and make a light roux. Add the beef stock gradually, stirring constantly. Cook for about five minutes. Add the spinach and onion and cook for another ten minutes. Sprinkle with grated Parmesan cheese just before serving. Serves 6.

*

*

COLD CHERRY SOUP
(Poland)

1 lb. cherries, pitted
½ tsp. cinnamon
1 c. sour cream

6 c. water
½ tsp. cloves
3 tbsp. flour

Soak the cherries in the water for about half an hour. Add in the cinnamon and cloves. Cook the cherries until tender. Save the water and pass the fruit through a sieve. Combine the flour and sour cream and add to the hot water and cherries. Bring to a boil, add the sugar and cook for about 15 minutes. Refrigerate before serving. Serves 6.

*

TARATOR
(Bulgaria)

2 cucumbers
4 c. yoghurt
½ c. walnuts, chopped
2 tbsp. lemon juice
1 c. cold water

2 tbsp. olive oil
1 tbsp. mint, finely diced
1 tbsp. dill, finely minced
2 cloves of garlic, minced
salt to taste

Peel and finely dice the cucumbers. Season with salt and refrigerate for about two hours. Combine the cucumbers with the lemon juice, water, olive oil, mint, dill, yoghurt, garlic and walnuts. Mash well or blend in a blender and chill for several hours. Garnish with freshly chopped parsley and halved or coarsely chopped walnuts. This makes an excellent cold summer soup. Serve over ice cubes. Serves 4.

*

COLD APPLE SOUP
(Russia)

4 baking apples	3 c. water
1 c. white wine	sugar to taste
½ tsp. cinnamon	¼ tsp. nutmeg
¼ tsp. allspice	1 lemon, sliced

Peel, core and coarsley chop the apples. Allow them to cook in the water until tender. Pass the apples through a sieve. Combine with the white wine. Stir well and add in as much sugar as desired. Add the seasonings and simmer over medium low heat for an additional five minutes. Refrigerate for a few hours. Garnish with lemon slices before serving. Serves 4.

*

---

*

LIVER DUMPLINGS
(Czechoslovakia)

¼ lb. liver
1 tsp. chopped garlic
1 egg

2 tbsp. butter
dash of marjoram
1 c. breadcrumbs
salt and pepper to taste

Clean and finely chop the liver. Cream the butter with the egg. Add in the liver, breadcrumbs and garlic. Season with marjoram, salt and pepper. Work this mixture into a dough. Add more breadcrumbs to thicken the dough if too soft. Use a teaspoon to break off the pieces of dough. Test the dough by placing a piece in boiling soup. If the dumpling does not break apart add in the rest of the dough. Allow dumplings to cook for 5 minutes. Serve soup hot.

*

EGG BALLS
(Poland)

2 hard-cooked eggs
2 egg yolks
salt and pepper to taste

1 tbsp. sour cream
1 tbsp. Parmesan cheese,
    grated

Mash the eggs and mix with the raw egg yolks. Add in the Parmesan cheese and season with salt and pepper. Mix in the sour cream and shape into balls. Drop the balls into the soup and allow to cook for a minute.

*

LIVER RICE
(Croatia)

1 c. cooked liver	3 tbsp. chopped onion
1 tbsp. lard or shortening	2 hard rolls
1 egg	1 tbsp. chopped parsley
2 tbsp. breadcrumbs	salt and pepper to taste

Saute the onion in one tablespoon of lard until golden brown. Soak the rolls in a little beef stock or milk then mash them. Add the egg, onion, parsley and mashed buns to the remaining lard. Mix well. Scrape the liver well, chop and add to the lard mixture. Season with salt and pepper. Add the breadcrumbs to this mixture and combine well. Grind the liver mixture in a grinder and add to boiling soup. Cook for a minute or two.

*

BUCKWHEAT KASHA
(Russia)

2 c. boiling water	¼ tsp. salt
½ c. buckwheat	

Add the buckwheat and salt to the water, stirring constantly. Cover the kasha and cook over low heat for 45 minutes. The kasha is ready when it is soft, but not mushy. This makes an excellent and nutritious soup additive.

*

DOUGH CRUMBLES
(The Ukraine)

1 c. flour

1 egg, well beaten
salt to taste

Work the flour into the beaten egg to make a stiff dough. Season the dough with salt and knead well. Grate the dough on a coarse grater. Set the crumbles aside to dry for two hours. Place the dough in boiling soup and cook for 10 minutes. This dough can be made days ahead of time and used all week.

*

SPOONED DUMPLINGS
(Croatia)

2 tbsp. butter
1 egg

3 tbsp. flour
dash of salt

Beat the butter well until it becomes light and frothy. Add the lightly beaten egg and flour and beat well with a spoon. Season with salt and continue beating a little longer. Spoon the dough into boiling soup and cook until tender.

*

BREAD DUMPLINGS
(Czechoslavakia)

1 tbsp. butter	⅓ c. breadcrumbs
1 egg, well beaten	2 tbsp. chopped parsley
	salt and pepper to taste

Cream the butter and add in the breadcrumbs, egg, parsley and salt and pepper. Make a firm dough. Shape the dough into balls. Cook for five minutes in hot soup or until the dumplings rise to the surface.

SEAFOODS

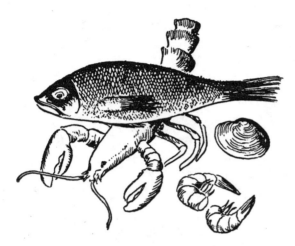

SEAFOODS

*

ROLLED HERRING
(Poland)

6 herring
1 onion, chopped
juice of one lemon
6 peppercorns
3 c. oil

2 tbsp. mustard
olive oil
3 bay leaves
2 c. milk
salt to taste

Remove the head and tail of each fish. Soak the herring in water, changing the water several times. Drain the herring and then soak in the milk. Remove the skin and split the fish down the middle. Remove the bones. Season with salt. Cover each fillet with mustard and chopped onion. Sprinkle with lemon juice. Roll up each herring and place in a bowl. Add the peppercorns and bay leaves, and pour in enough oil to cover the herring. Refrigerate the fish for three days and then serve garnished with lemon slices. Serves 4.

*

*

WHITEFISH IN WINE
(Croatia)

2 lbs. whitefish fillets
½ lb. sliced potatoes
1½ c. mushrooms, thinly
   sliced

3 tbsp. butter
¾ c. white wine
1 c. sour cream
salt to taste

Butter a deep baking dish and place a layer of potatoes in it. Dab chunks of butter over the potatoes. Cover them with half the cream. Heat the wine and cook the mushrooms in it for five to ten minutes. Pour this over the sour cream. Add the fillets and season with salt. Add the remaining potatoes. Cover with the remaining cream. Bake at 375° for about half an hour or until the potatoes are tender. Serves 4.

*

BOILED PIKE
(Czechoslovakia)

1 medium pike
1 onion, finely chopped
¾ c. horseradish, grated
juice of ½ a lemon

2 carrots, sliced
2 tsp. parsley
¾ c. cream
2 tsp. sugar

Clean the pike and place in a pan. Cover with salted water and add in the carrots, parsley and onion. Simmer the fish with the vegetables for half an hour to 45 minutes until the fish is tender. Combine the horseradish and cream. Add the lemon juice and sugar. Blend well and pour over the boiled pike. Serves 4.

*

WALNUT-STUFFED CARP
(Bulgaria)

1 3-lb. carp
1 onion, finely chopped
1 clove of garlic, finely
  chopped

3 tbsp. olive oil
1 c. chopped walnuts
½ c. raisins, soaked in milk
salt and pepper to taste

Soak the carp in fresh water for several hours. Remove the carp from the water and season with salt. Heat the olive oil and saute the onion, walnuts and garlic for five minutes. Add the raisins and season with salt and pepper. Cover the onions and raisins and cook for another five minutes. Stuff the fish with this mixture. Coat with additional olive oil and bake in a moderate oven at 350° for about an hour and a half or until well done. Serves 4.

*

*

CABBAGE AND CARP
(Poland)

1 whole carp	1 tbsp. butter
2 lbs. red cabbage	1 tbsp. flour
1 onion, finely chopped	1 c. red wine
1 tbsp. sugar	1 tbsp. vinegar
	salt and pepper to taste

Shred the cabbage. Soak the carp in fresh water for several hours. Cut the fish into steaks. Boil the cabbage in salted water for a minute. Heat the butter in a skillet. Add the onion and brown it in the butter. Add the flour, red wine, sugar, vinegar and the cabbage. Season with salt and pepper. Cook for fifteen minutes over low heat. Add the carp steaks and simmer for half an hour. Season again with salt and pepper. Shake the pan occasionally to prevent sticking. Serve on a warmed platter. Serves 4-5.

*

PIKE WITH VEGETABLES
(Bulgaria)

2 lbs. pike fillets	½ c. celery, diced
1 carrot, sliced	3 tomatoes
4 onions, finely chopped	1 c. olive oil
3 cloves garlic, chopped	juice ½ lemon

½ c. white wine
½ c. ground walnuts

2 bay leaves
salt and pepper to taste

Peel and slice the tomatoes. Combine the vegetables, and garlic and place the mixture in a greased casserole dish. Season with salt and pepper. Add the fish and cover with white wine, lemon juice, bay leaves and walnuts. Pour the olive oil over the fish and season with salt and pepper. Cover the casserole dish and place in a moderate oven at 350° for about one hour and a half. Serves 4-5.

*

CHAMPAGNE CARP
(Croatia)

2 lbs. carp
1 c. champagne
½ lb. mushrooms, sliced
2 egg yolks, well beaten

4 tbsp. butter
2 tbsp. flour
1 c. sour cream

Clean the carp and cut into steaks. Place the fish in a saucepan and pour the champagne over it. Allow the fish to simmer until most of the champagne has disappeared. Heat the butter and saute the mushrooms in it for five or ten minutes. Stir in the cream, flour and the egg yolks. Pour this sauce over the fish and bake the carp in the oven at 400° for fifteen minutes. Serves 4-5.

*

*

PAPRIKA COD
(Slovenia)

2 lbs. filleted cod
2 potatoes
2 green peppers
1 bay leaf
2 tbsp. oil

2 onions, finely chopped
2 tomatoes
2 cloves garlic, minced
1 tbsp. paprika
4 c. water
salt and pepper to taste

Peel the potatoes and the tomatoes. Cube the potatoes and chop the tomatoes and green peppers. Heat the oil in a saucepan. Add the onions and garlic and saute for five minutes, stirring constantly. Add the peppers, tomatoes, potatoes, paprika and bay leaf. Season with salt and pepper. Slowly add in the water. Allow the vegetables to cook for half an hour. Fish bones and trimmings may be added to the vegetables for added flavor. If bones are added, remove when vegetables are cooked. Mash the vegetables when cooked to form a thin vegetable puree. Place the fish fillets in a baking dish and coat with oil. Sprinkle generously with paprika and season with salt and pepper. Pour in the vegetable puree. Bake in a moderate oven at 350° for 45 minutes. Baste with more oil as required. Place the fish on a warmed platter and serve hot. Serves 4.

*

*

BOILED SALMON
(Russia)

1 2-lb salmon
1 onion, finely chopped
¼ c. celery, diced
3 green onions
4 peppercorns
¾ c. cream
2 tsp. sugar

1 bay leaf
½ tsp. dill, finely chopped
½ tsp. chopped parsley
5 c. water
¾ c. horseradish, grated
juice of half a lemon
salt to taste

Wash the salmon and clean it. Season the fish with salt and refrigerate for an hour. Finely chop the green onion. Heat the water in a large pot and add the onion, green onion, celery, bayleaf, dill, peppercorns and parsley. Bring to a boil. Add the salmon and season with salt. Cook the fish for 45 minutes over low heat or until the fish is tender. When the salmon is done, remove gently and place on a warm platter. Combine the grated horseradish, cream, sugar and lemon juice to make a sauce. Blend well and pour over the salmon just before serving. Serves 4-5.

*

EEL IN WINE
(Poland)

2 lbs. eel
1 onion, finely chopped

2 tbsp. butter
½ c. white wine

1 c. water
1 clove of garlic, minced

½ c. mushrooms
salt and pepper to taste

Skin and slice the eel. Heat the butter in a saucepan and saute the onion and garlic in it for five minutes. Add the eel, mushrooms, wine and water. Season with salt and pepper. Allow the eel to cook over low heat for half an hour or until tender. Serve on a heated platter covered with the sauce in which it was cooked. Serves 4.

*

BOILED CHRISTMAS CARP
(Czechoslovakia)

1 3-lb carp
3 c. water
¼ c. celery, diced
1 carrot, sliced
1 parsnip, diced
1 onion, finely chopped
2 tbsp. butter

1 bay leaf
½ c. vinegar
8 peppercorns
1 tsp. chopped parsley
lemon wedges
salt to taste

Soak the carp in fresh water for several hours. Clean the fish and split it. Heat the water and add the carrot, parsnip, celery, bay leaf, peppercorns and onion. Allow the vegetables to cook for fifteen minutes. Bring the vinegar to a boil. Place the carp in a pan and scald the skin with hot vinegar. The skin should turn dark blue. Slowly add the vegetables and water. Season with salt. Allow the fish to cook for half an hour, covered. Place the carp on a warm platter and pour the melted butter over it. Sprinkle with parsley and serve with lemon wedges. Serves 4-5.

*

BROILED FISH ROE
(Slovenia)

2 lbs. fish roe
1 tsp. lemon juice

1 tsp. chopped parsley
salt and pepper to taste

Boil the fish roe in salted water for five to ten minutes. Remove from water and break into pieces. Place on a greased baking dish. Sprinkle the parsley and lemon juice over the roe. Season with pepper. Place under the broiler for about ten minutes. Serves 4.

*

PERCH IN WHITE WINE
(Poland)

2 lbs. perch fillets
1½ c. white wine
1 onion, finely chopped
lemon slices

2 tbsp. dill, finely chopped
3 tbsp. butter
2 eggs, well beaten
salt and pepper to taste

Heat the butter in a saucepan and saute the onion in it until tender. Add the wine, dill, salt and pepper. Bring the wine to a boil and add the perch fillets. Simmer the fillets for fifteen minutes. Pour in the beaten eggs slowly. Cook the fillets for another five minutes. Serve with lemon slices. Serves 4.

*

*

DALMATIAN BRODET
(Croatia)

2 lbs. assorted salt water
   fish fillets
1 clove garlic, chopped
1 tbsp. chopped parsley
½ lb. tomatoes
   or 1 c. tomato sauce

1 c. wine
1/4 c. olive oil
3 tbsp. flour
3 tbsp. butter
½ c. sliced onion
salt and pepper to taste

Clean the fish and cut it into fairly large steaks. Season with salt and pepper. Roll the steaks in the flour and fry them in the hot olive oil. Melt the butter over low heat. Increase the heat and brown the onions in the butter. Add the parsley, garlic, wine and the sliced tomatoes or tomato sauce. Simmer slowly for about half an hour. Add the fish and enough water to cover. Continue to simmer for another half hour or until the fish is tender. Do not stir; instead, shake the pan occasionally. This will prevent the fish from sticking, yet will keep it from breaking apart. Carefully arrange the steaks on a serving platter. Cover with the tomato and onion sauce. Serves 4-5.

*

*

BREADED COD
(Poland)

2 lb. filleted cod   ¼ c. flour
3 eggs, well beaten   ¼ c. breadcrumbs
¼ c. butter   salt and pepper to taste

Season the flour with salt and pepper. Melt the butter in a saucepan or skillet. Dredge the pieces of cod in flour, then dip them in the eggs and roll in breadcrumbs. Heat the butter so it is hot. Add the fish and fry until golden brown. Serve with potatoes and cabbage. Serves 4.

*

GRILLED SALMON
(Russia)

2 lbs. salmon steaks   1/4 c. olive oil
                      salt and pepper to taste

Salt the steaks and refrigerate for about an hour. Wipe the steaks with a towel. Grease a grill with the olive oil. Coat the fish steaks with olive oil and season with salt and pepper. Place the fish on the grill and grill until well browned. Turn the fish over and grill the other side. Serve with potatoes or rice. Serves 4.

*

*

BAKED TROUT
(The Ukraine)

10 trout
1 tbsp. parsley

4 tbsp. melted butter
5 tbsp. breadcrumbs
salt and pepper to taste

Pour the butter into a baking dish. Wash and clean the trout and cut off the heads and tails. Coat the fish with melted butter and season with salt and pepper. Sprinkle with breadcrumbs. Brush the breadcrumbs with butter. Sprinkle with parsley and bake the trout in a moderate oven at 350° for one hour or until well browned. Serves 5-6.

*

CODFISH BALLS
(Croatia)

2 c. cooked cod
1 c. mashed potatoes
3 tbsp. milk
oil for deep frying

3 tbsp. olive oil
2 eggs, well beaten
1 tbsp. lemon juice
salt and pepper to taste

Combine the cod and potatoes with the milk, lemon juice and olive oil, and mash well. Stir in the eggs and season with salt and pepper. When the mixture is well combined, shape into balls. Deep fry in oil until the balls are a golden brown. Serves 4.

*

MACKEREL WITH SAUERKRAUT
(Bulgaria)

2 lbs. mackerel fillets   ½ c. olive oil
2 lbs. sauerkraut   2 tsp. paprika
1 clove garlic, minced   ¼ c. breadrumbs
                              salt and pepper to taste

Heat half the olive oil and saute the sauerkraut for ten minutes. Season with salt and pepper. Place the sauerkraut in a casserole dish and sprinkle with one teaspoon paprika and the breadcrumbs. Add the fish fillets. Season with salt and pepper and sprinkle with the remaining teaspoon of paprika and with the garlic. Coat the fillets with olive oil and bake in a moderate oven at 350° until the fish is cooked, about half an hour. Serves 4-5.

*

COOKED CRAYFISH
(The Ukraine)

10 crayfish   1 tbsp. dill, finely chopped
1 carrot, sliced   1 bay leaf
1 onion, chopped   5 c. water
                              salt and pepper to taste

Wash the crayfish and place them in a saucepan. Add the

carrot, onion, bay leaf, dill and water. Season with salt and pepper. Cook until the vegetables and the crayfish are tender. Serve the crayfish with the vegetable sauce. Serves 4-5.

*

STURGEON WITH SOUR CREAM
(Poland)

1 medium sturgeon   2 carrots, sliced
1 onion, finely chopped   3 tbsp. butter
1 tbsp. flour   2 tsp. chopped parsley
1 c. sour cream

Wash the sturgeon and scald with boiling water. Clean the fish and remove the skin. Season the fish with salt. Heat the butter in a skillet and brown the onion in it. Add the carrots, the sturgeon, and enough water to cover. Allow to cook for half an hour or until tender. Add the sour cream and the flour and cook for an additional minute or two. Garnish with parsley and serve. Serves 4-6.

*

*

SKEWERED SWORDFISH
(Croatia)

1½ lbs. swordfish steaks
¼ c. olive oil
2 tbsp. chopped onion
juice of one lemon

10 bay leaves
1 tbsp. chopped parsley
½ tsp. paprika
1½ tsp. salt
½ tsp. pepper

Cube the fish into bite-sized chunks. Combine the remaining ingredients. Place the fish cubes into this marinade and refrigerate overnight. The following day, remove the fish from the marinade, drain and place on skewers. Grill over hot coals for about fifteen minutes, turning occasionally. Serve with a tangy lemon sauce. Serves 4.

POULTRY
AND
GAME

POULTRY AND GAME

*

PODVARKA
(Croatia)

1 medium turkey	¼ c. butter
1 turkey liver	2 lbs. sauerkraut
1 tsp. paprika	4 potatoes, grated
2 c. coarse breadcrumbs	2 onions, grated
1 c. sour cream	salt and pepper to taste

Season the turkey very well inside and out with salt, pepper and paprika. Refrigerate for at least two or three hours. Melt the butter over medium heat. Increase the heat. Add the sauerkraut, potatoes, onions and pepper to taste. Cook for approximately ten minutes, stirring constantly. Finely chop the turkey liver. Combine it with the breadcrumbs and sour cream and mix well. Stuff the turkey with this mixture. Close the opening with thread or metal skewers. Combine the sauerkraut, grated potatoes and grated onion. Spread the sauerkraut and potato mixture in the bottom of a well-greased roasting pan. Place the turkey on top of the sauerkraut mixture and roast uncovered in a 350° oven. Allow the turkey to roast for 20 minutes per pound of weight. Baste frequently with melted butter. Turn the turkey several times while roasting. Roast the bird with the breast upward during the last half hour. Serve hot on the bed of cooked sauerkraut. Serves 7-8.

81

*

ROAST SQUAB
(Czechoslovakia)

6 squabs
1 c. butter
6 squab livers, chopped
2 c. breadcrumbs
½ c. warm milk

4 eggs, well beaten
1 onion, finely chopped
2 tbsp. chopped parsley
½ tsp. mace
salt and pepper to taste

Soak the breadcrumbs in the warm milk. Cream half the butter with the eggs and season with salt and pepper. Add the breadcrumbs and milk, onion, mace, parsley and liver. Mix well and season once again. Clean the squabs and salt the cavity. Stuff the squabs with the stuffing. Season the birds with salt and pepper. Melt the remaining butter and pour over the birds coating them well. Roast the squabs in a moderate oven at 350° for 30-40 minutes. Add water as required while the squabs roast, and baste frequently. Allow them to turn a golden brown and then serve. Serves 6.

*

BRAISED DUCK WITH MUSHROOMS
(Poland)

1 4-lb. duck
1 onion, finely chopped
½ tsp. thyme

4 c. water
½ lb. mushrooms, sliced
2 tbsp. chopped parsley

---

4 tbsp. flour
¼ c. bacon fat
2 tbsp. butter

4 apples, cored and
    quartered
salt and pepper to taste

Wash the duck and season with salt and pepper. Stuff the duck with the apples and roast in a moderate oven at 350° for two hours. When the duck is done remove and discard the apples. Heat the bacon fat and saute the duck until brown. Add the onion, thyme and parsley. Season with salt and pepper and cover the duck with the water. Allow to cook for another 20 minutes. Saute the mushrooms in the butter until they turn brown. Slowly stir in the flour and allow to brown. Pour in stock slowly to make a sauce. Place the duck on a warmed platter and pour the mushroom sauce over it. Serves 4.

*

ROAST GOOSE AND CABBAGE
(Russia)

1 8-lb. goose, cut into
    pieces
2 tbsp. butter, melted

1 head of cabbage
3 onions, sliced
salt and pepper to taste

Place the pieces of goose in a roasting pan and season with salt and pepper. Pour the melted butter over the goose. Add half a cup of water and roast for three hours in a moderate oven at 350°. Chop the cabbage coarsley. Heat six tablespoons of fat from the goose and saute the onion and cabbage in it. Season with salt and pepper. Cook the cabbage and onion for another ten minutes. Place the

---

pieces of goose on top of the cabbage and cover tightly. Allow the goose and cabbage to simmer for another hour or until the goose is tender. Serves 7-8

*

CHICKEN WITH WINE SAUCE
(Bulgaria)

1 chicken, cut into pieces	1 c. white wine
1 c. olive oil	2 onions, sliced
¼ c. tomato sauce	2 tbsp. flour
½ tsp. paprika	2 cloves garlic, minced
3 tbsp. water	salt and pepper to taste

Heat the olive oil in a saucepan and saute the garlic and onions. Stir in the tomato sauce and the wine slowly. Add the chicken and allow to cook covered for two hours or until the chicken is tender. Combine the flour, water and paprika. Season with salt and pepper. Add this to the chicken and allow to cook until the sauce thickens. Serve on a heated platter with the sauce. Serves 5-6.

*

ROAST CAPON WITH CHESTNUT STUFFING
(Czechoslovakia)

1 capon (5-6 pounds)	1 c. cooked chestnuts
¼ c. breadcrumbs	½ c. butter

½ onion, finely chopped
bacon for larding

2 tbsp. cream
salt and pepper to taste

Clean the bird well and lard the breast with the bacon. To lard the bird, cut the bacon into strips and insert into gashes in the meat of the bird or use a larding needle to pull the bacon into the lean meat. Mash the chestnuts and combine with half the butter, the breadcrumbs, cream and onion. Season with salt and pepper. Stuff the capon with this stuffing and sew up the cavity. Place in a roasting pan, melt the remaining butter and pour over the bird. Add a cup of water. Sprinkle salt and pepper over the capon and roast in a moderate oven at 350° for two to three hours. Add water when necessary and baste frequently. Serves 6.

*

CHICKEN KIEV
(The Ukraine)

6 chicken breasts, boned
1 c. butter, refrigerated
½ onion, finely chopped
¾ c. breadcrumbs

4 eggs, well beaten
¼ c. mushrooms, chopped
1 tsp. chopped parsley
salt and pepper to taste

Pound the breasts out flat with a meat tenderizer and cut in half lengthwise. Break the butter into small pieces and place in the freezer until hardened. Place a few pieces of butter, mushrooms, and onion on each of the chicken breasts and fold over the breasts and fasten with toothpicks so that the butter can't leak out. Season the breadcrumbs with salt and pepper and roll the breasts in the breadcrumbs. Then roll the _breasts in egg and once again in the breadcrumbs. Heat oil for deep frying and fry the chicken breasts until golden brown. Drain the cutlets and serve garnished with parsley. Serves 6._

*

TURKEY WITH SAUSAGE STUFFING
(Poland)

1 turkey
2 c. breadcrumbs
½ onion, finely chopped
bacon for larding

½ lb. Polish sausage,
   finely chopped
1 tbsp. chopped parsley
1 turkey liver, chopped
salt and pepper to taste

Clean the turkey and salt the cavity. Lard the bird by cutting the bacon into strips and inserting into gashes in the meat of the bird, or use a larding needle to pull the bacon into the lean meat. Combine the sausage, breadcrumbs, parsley, turkey liver and onion. Season with salt and pepper and mix well. Stuff the turkey with this mixture. Place the bird in a roasting pan and coat with melted butter. Add a cup of water and cover with foil. Bake the turkey in a moderate oven at 350° for five to six hours, basting frequently. When done, remove the foil and turn up the heat. Continue to bake for another ten to fifteen minutes to brown the skin. Serves 7-8.

*

*

ROAST VENISON
(Slovenia)

5-6 lbs. venison
1 onion, finely chopped
bacon for larding
1 tbsp. flour
2 cups sour cream
2 tbsp. butter, melted

2 c. wine vinegar
1 bay leaf
2 cloves garlic, chopped
4 peppercorns
1 tbsp. chopped parsley
salt and pepper to taste

Combine the wine vinegar, bay leaf, peppercorns, garlic, onion and parsley. Season with salt. Pour this over the venison and refrigerate overnight. The following day, drain the meat and lard with the bacon. To lard the meat, cut the bacon into strips and insert into gashes in the meat or use a larding needle to pull the bacon into the lean meat. Place the meat in a roasting pan and pour the melted butter over the meat. Allow the meat to roast for five to six hours until tender. Add water as necessary and baste often. Mix together the sour cream and flour. Season with salt and pepper. Pour the sour cream over the venison and allow to roast for another three to five minutes. Serve with the meat's juices. Serves 8-10.

*

*

CHICKEN AND DUMPLINGS
(Poland)

1 chicken, cut into pieces	3 tbsp. flour
2 tsp. baking powder	1½ c. milk
1 c. flour	1 egg, beaten
1 tsp. salt	salt and pepper to taste

Sift one cup of flour with the baking powder. Combine the salt, ½ cup of milk and the beaten egg. Stir in the sifted flour slowly and beat into a smooth dough. Place the chicken in a pot and cover with salted water. Cook for one to two hours if the chicken is young, and three to four hours for an older chicken. Twenty minutes before the chicken is done, add the dumplings by breaking the dough off with a spoon. Remove the dumplings from the stock when done and set aside in a warmed dish. Mix together the three tablespoons of flour and the remaining milk to make a paste. Add this paste to the chicken stock and cook over medium heat long enough to make a medium gravy. Season with salt and pepper. Take the chicken out and place it on a warmed serving platter. Place the dumplings on and around the chicken and pour the gravy on top. Serves 5-6.

*

CHICKEN WITH CHESTNUT AND TOMATO SAUCE
(Bulgaria)

1 chicken, cut into pieces	4 tbsp. tomato sauce
1 lb. chestnuts, shelled	4 tbsp. olive oil

2 onions, finely chopped   3 tbsp. water
½ tsp. paprika   salt and pepper to taste

Boil the chestnuts in salted water until tender. Remove from water, drain and mash the chestnuts. Heat the olive oil in a saucepan. Add the chicken and onions and saute for five to ten minutes. Add the tomato sauce, water, paprika and mashed chestnuts. Season the chicken with salt and pepper. Cover the pan and allow to cook for two hours. Shake the pan occasionally to prevent sticking. Serves 4-5.

*

FRIED GOOSE LIVER
(Russia)

2 lb. goose liver, chopped   1 onion, finely chopped
2 tbsp. flour   2 c. milk
4 tbsp. butter   ½ c. mushrooms, sliced
    salt and pepper to taste

Place the livers in the milk and allow to soak for an hour. Remove from the milk and dust with the flour. Heat the butter in a skillet and add the goose liver, onion and mushroooms. Saute the livers so that they brown, but allow them to remain slightly pink on the inside. Season with salt and pepper. Serves 4.

*

*

CHICKEN IN SOUR CREAM
(The Ukraine)

1 chicken, cut into pieces	4 tbsp. butter
2 c. sour cream	1 c. mushrooms, sliced
4 tbsp. flour	1 chopped onion
2 cloves of garlic, minced	salt and pepper to taste

Heat the butter in a saucepan. Add the chicken and garlic. Saute the chicken until golden-brown. Add the onion and mushrooms and saute for another fifteen minutes. Remove the chicken and stir in the flour and sour cream. Season with salt and pepper. Mix well and replace the chicken. Cover and simmer over low heat for 20 minutes. Serves 4-5.

*

CHICKEN WITH WALNUT SAUCE
(Russia)

1 chicken, cut into pieces	3 tbsp. oil
2 cloves garlic, chopped	2 tbsp. flour
1 c. chicken stock	½ c. walnuts, ground
1 onion, finely chopped	¼ tsp. nutmeg
¼ tsp. cinnamon	salt and pepper to taste

Dredge the chicken in flour and season with salt and pepper. Heat the oil in a saucepan and add half the garlic and the chicken. *Cover and cook the chicken for half an hour. Remove the chicken and add the remaining garlic, onion and walnuts. Saute for five minutes. Add one tablespoon of flour. Mix well and allow the flour to brown. Pour in the chicken stock and add the nutmeg and cinnamon. Season with salt and pepper. Allow this to cook until a medium sauce has formed, stirring constantly. Pour this sauce over the warm chicken and serve. Serves 4-5.*

*

BREADED TURKEY CUTLETS
(Croatia)

1½ lbs. turkey breast
¼ c. flour
2 eggs

¾ c. breadcrumbs
½ c. butter
½ c. oil
salt and pepper to taste

After removing the tendons from the meat, pound it with a meat tenderizer until it is no more than ¼ inch in thickness. Season the flour with the salt and pepper. Beat the eggs with a little water. Heat the butter and oil. Roll the meat slices in the flour, dip in egg and coat with breadcrumbs. Fry immediately so that the coating does not fall off. Fry in the hot fat on both sides until they become a light golden color. Serves 6.

*

*

ROAST GOOSE
(Czechoslovakia)

1 medium goose   2 tsp. caraway seeds
2 c. water   salt and pepper to taste
2 tbsp. butter, melted

Wash the goose and place in a roasting pan. Season with salt and pepper. Pour the melted butter over the goose. Add the water and caraway seeds. Pierce the skin of the goose, cover the bird with foil and roast in the oven at 350° for three hours. Baste the bird frequently while roasting. Remove the foil, increase the temperature and roast for another ten to fifteen minutes to brown the skin. Serves 6-8.

*

ROAST PIGEON
(Poland)

4 pigeons   2 tbsp. butter, melted
bacon for larding   salt and pepper to taste

Wash the pigeons and soak in cold water for about an hour. Remove from the water, drain and lard the birds by cutting the bacon into strips and inserting into gashes in the meat of the bird or use a larding needle to pull the bacon into the lean meat. Place the birds in a roasting pan and season with salt and pepper. Pour the melted butter over the birds. Roast the pigeons in the oven at 350° for about half an hour, basting frequently. Serves 4.

*

DUCK WITH OLIVES
(Bulgaria)

1 duck, cut into pieces	1 tbsp. flour
1 onion, finely chopped	½ c. wine
¼ c. olive oil	2 cloves garlic, minced
1 c. black olives, pitted	salt and pepper to taste

Heat the olive oil in a saucepan and add the garlic, duck and onion. Saute the duck until brown. Add the wine, flour and olives. Season with salt and pepper. Allow to cook slowly over medium heat until tender. Serves 4.

*

PIGEON WITH MUSHROOMS
(Czechoslovakia)

6 pigeons, cut into pieces	2 tbsp. oil
1 c. mushrooms, sliced	5 tbsp. tomato puree
4 c. meat stock	4 tbsp. cream
2 onions, finely chopped	salt and pepper to taste

Heat the oil in a saucepan and add the pigeons. Saute for five to ten minutes. Stir in the tomato puree and meat stock. Season with salt and pepper. Allow to simmer for an hour. Add the mushrooms and onions and cook for an additional fifteen minutes. When cooked, stir in the cream and serve. Serves 7-8.

*

CHICKEN À LA BAČKA
(Croatia)

1 large fryer, pieced
¼ c. lard or shortening
¼ c. bacon, diced
½ tsp. paprika
2 tomatoes, sliced

2-3 green peppers, cut
   into strips
2 c. chicken stock
1 small bunch parsley
1 onion, finely chopped
salt and pepper to taste

Saute the onion and the bacon in 3 tbsp. lard or shortening until the onion browns slightly. Season with paprika. Stir and add a little water. Place the chicken pieces in this mixture. Season with salt and pepper. Stir occassionaly, adding a little water each time. Cook over low heat for about 45 minutes. Prepare the vegetables. Add the vegetables to the chicken and stir well. Add the chicken stock and bring to a boil. Reduce the heat and simmer slowly for another half hour until the vegetables are tender, but do not overcook. Be careful that the chicken does not break away from the bones when it is placed in a serving dish. Cover with the sauce that the chicken was cooked in. Sprinkle with parsley and garnish with fresh tomato slices and pepper rings, if desired. Serves 6.

*

DUCK WITH ONIONS
(Czechoslovakia)

1 duck, cut into pieces
2 onions, cut into rings
½ c. water

4 tbsp. butter
2 clove garlic, minced
dash of paprika
salt and pepper to taste

Heat the butter in a skillet and saute the garlic quickly. Add the pieces of duck and half the water. Season with salt and pepper. Allow to cook for half an hour. Stir in the remaining water and cook for another half an hour. Add in the onions and season with salt. Cook for another half an hour or until onions are tender. Season with paprika and serve. Serves 4.

*

ROAST RABBIT WITH SOUR CREAM
(Poland)

1 rabbit
2 c. sour cream
2 tsp. parsley
  finely minced

2 tbsp. butter, melted
1 tbsp. flour
bacon for larding
salt and pepper to taste

Clean and lard the rabbit by cutting bacon into strips and inserting into gashes in the meat of the rabbit, or use a larding needle to pull the bacon into the lean meat. Place the rabbit in a roasting pan and season with salt and pepper. Pour the melted butter over the rabbit and add ½ cup water. Bake the rabbit in a moderate oven at 350° for one hour, basting often. Combine the parsley, sour cream and flour. Season with salt and pepper. Pour the sour cream mixture over the rabbit and allow to roast an additional three to five minutes. Serve the rabbit with the juices in which it was roasted. Serves 4-5.

CASSEROLES

CASSEROLES

*

SARMA
(Croatia)

2 heads pickled cabbage
1 lb. ground beef
1 lb. smoked ham, diced
¼ c. smoked bacon, diced
2 tbsp. flour
1 egg

1 c. rice
2 tsp. paprika
1 onion, chopped
2 tbsp. shortening
salt and pepper to taste

Fry the bacon in its own fat. Add the onion and the ground beef and fry for about five minutes. Remove from heat, drain the excess fat and allow to cool slightly. Add the chopped ham, rice, egg, 1 tsp. paprika, salt and pepper. Mix well. Remove the large outer leaves of the cabbage. Cut off the outer ribs. Place some filling in each cabbage leaf and roll it up from the center of the leaf to the outer edge. Tuck the sides into the center to hold the roll together. Cut any remaining cabbage into strips. If desired, add another half pound of sauerkraut. Place half the sauerkraut in the bottom of a large Dutch oven pot. Arrange the cabbage rolls over the sauerkraut. Cover with the remaining sauerkraut. Melt the shortening and heat until it becomes very hot. Brown the flour in the hot shortening. Add 1 tsp. paprika and enough water to make a thick roux. Cook for five minutes. Pour the roux over the cabbage rolls. Add enough water to cover and simmer over low heat for 1½ to 2 hours until the rice is fully cooked. Do not stir the rolls while they

---

are cooking, instead, shake the pot occasionally to prevent sticking. Makes approximately two dozen cabbage rolls. Serves 8-10.

Since pickled cabbage is not readily available in the United States, this recipe can also be made using fresh cabbage. Bring a pot of salted water to boil. Remove from the stove and place the cabbage in it. Allow the cabbage to soak in the hot water for approximately an hour to soften the leaves. Stuff the leaves with the meat and rice mixture. When the cabbage rolls are prepared, alternate layers of cabbage rolls and layers of sauerkraut using 2 pounds of sauerkraut.

*

MUTTON GOULASH
(Czechoslovakia)

1½ lbs. mutton, cubed
1 carrot, sliced
3 c. water
¼ c. celery root, diced
1 onion, finely chopped
1 c. kale, chopped
3 potatoes, peeled

½ c. bacon, diced
1 parsnip, diced
1 clove garlic, finely diced
¼ tsp. marjoram
¼ tsp. caraway seeds
salt and pepper to taste

Place the bacon and garlic in a skillet and heat for five minutes. Add the carrot, onion, parsnip, celery root and mutton. Saute for an additional five minutes. Pour in a cup of water and allow the meat and vegetables to simmer for an hour and a half. Season the stew with salt, pepper, marjoram and caraway seeds. Stir and add the cubed potatoes, the kale and the remaining water. Cover and cook for another half hour. Serves 4.

*

RUSSIAN BEEF CASSEROLE
(Russia)

2 lb. steak, cubed
6 tbsp. butter
2 c. sour cream
½ c. cooked peas

¾ lb. mushrooms, sliced
2 tbsp. flour
2 onions, finely chopped
1 clove of garlic, minced
salt and pepper to taste

Heat 2 tbsp. butter in a saucepan and brown the beef in it. Season with salt and pepper. Heat 2 tbsp. butter in another saucepan and saute the mushrooms, garlic and onions for five to ten minutes. Butter a casserole dish and place a layer of beef on the bottom. Mix the cooked peas with the mushrooms and place a layer over the beef. Continue layering until the meat and mushrooms are used up, leaving the top layer meat. Melt the remaining butter and stir in the flour and sour cream. Blend well and pour over the casserole. Bake in a moderate oven at 350° for 45 minutes. Serve with kasha *or noodles. Serves 6.*

*

MUSHROOM CASSEROLE
(Czechoslovakia)

2½ lbs. mushrooms, sliced
1 onion, finely chopped

5 large potatoes, peeled
½ c. butter

1 c. milk
1 clove garlic, diced

2 eggs, well beaten
salt and pepper to taste

Heat the butter in a saucepan and saute the mushrooms, onion, and garlic for five minutes. Season with salt and pepper. Boil the potatoes in salted water until cooked. Drain and slice the potatoes. Butter a casserole dish and place a layer of potatoes on the bottom and then a layer of mushrooms and onion. Continue layering until potatoes and mushrooms are used up. Combine the milk and eggs and pour over the mushrooms and potatoes. Bake in a moderate oven at 350° for half an hour. Serves 6.

*

KULEBIAKA
(Russia)

Pastry:

3 c. flour
juice of ½ a lemon

½ c. ice water
1½ c. butter, refrigerated

Sift the flour twice. Add the lemon juice. Work in the cold butter with a pastry cutter until the butter and four have combined into flakes. Pour the ice water into the flour and butter immediately and work into a ball. If the dough crumbles, add a little more ice water. Cut the dough in half and refrigerate for 2-3 hours. It is essential that all ingredients and utensils be kept very cold.

Filling:

3 lbs. salmon
¼ c. butter
1 c. mushrooms, sliced
2 hard-cooked eggs, chopped
1 c. white wine

juice of ½ lemon
2 onions, finely chopped
8 peppercorns
½ c. cooked rice
4 tbsp. dill, finely chopped
salt and pepper to taste

Clean and salt the salmon. Place the fish in salted water and add the white wine and peppercorns. Cook the fish for fifteen minutes. Drain, remove the bones and flake the fish. Heat the butter in a saucepan and saute the onions and mushrooms for five minutes in it; add the dill and season with salt and pepper. Pour the lemon juice over the mushrooms when sauted. Combine the salmon, rice, mushrooms and onions and hard-cooked eggs. Mix well and season with salt and pepper. Roll out the dough balls until they are 1/8 inch thick and twice as long as they are wide. Place the dough on a greased baking sheet and cut straight edges. Place the filling on top of the first piece of dough, the whole length. Take the remaining dough and place on top of the filling. Pinch together the edges of the two sheets of dough after wetting them. Use any remaining dough as decoration by cutting out with a cookie cutter various designs such as leaves or stars. Prick the dough with a fork to allow air to circulate while baking, and coat with beaten eggs. Refrigerate the kulebiaka for half an hour before baking. Bake in a hot oven at 450° for ten minutes, then lower the heat to 400° and bake for 35-45 minutes until golden brown. Serves 6.

✱

*

LAMB AND LEEK STEW
(Russia)

2½ lbs. lamb, cubed   2 c. leeks, sliced
2 tbsp. oil   1 onion, sliced
1 clove of garlic, minced   2 eggs, well beaten
1 tbsp. lemon juice   3 c. water
                            salt and pepper to taste

Heat the oil in a saucepan and brown the lamb in it. Add the onion, garlic and leeks and saute for five minutes. Season with salt and pepper. Stir in the water and allow the meat and leeks to cook for one and a half hours. Just before serving, combine the eggs and lemon juice and add to the stew. Cook a few minutes longer and serve. Serves 6.

*

PORK WITH SAUERKRAUT
(The Ukraine)

2 lbs. pork   4 c. sauerkraut
1 c. barley   1 bay leaf
                    salt and pepper to taste

Cut the meat into large chunks and place in a casserole or Dutch oven. Wash the sauerkraut and drain. Add to the pork along with the barley and bay leaf, and season with salt and pepper. Add enough water to cover. Cover the casserole and allow to simmer for two hours. Serves 6.

*

HUNTING PIE
(Poland)

2½ lbs. veal
2 carrots, sliced
1 tsp. parsley, chopped
½ c. white wine
½ c. shortening
¼ tsp. salt

1 c. celery, diced
1 onion, finely chopped
3 tbsp. butter
1 c. flour, sifted
3 tbsp. cold water
salt and pepper to taste

Pour the flour in a bowl and place in the refrigerator. Also keep the shortening in the refrigerator. Melt 3 tbsp. of butter in a saucepan and saute the veal in it. Season with salt, pepper and parsley. Place the veal and the vegetables in a greased casserole dish. Pour in the white wine and mix well. To make the crust, sift the flour and salt together and cut in the shortening with a knife or pastry cutter. Slowly add a little cold water at a time, mixing together to form a dough. It is necessary for the dough to remain cold so that it will remain flaky. Roll the dough out on a floured board. Place the dough on the top and the sides of the meat and vegetable mixture in the casserole dish. Prick the top dough with a fork to make air holes. Place in the oven and bake at 450° for ten minutes. Reduce the heat and bake at 350° for another 20 to 25 minutes. Serves 6.

*

*

RABBIT CASSEROLE
(Russia)

1 rabbit, cut into pieces
2 carrots, sliced
2 onions, finely chopped
1 c. vinegar
1 bay leaf
2 c. water

2 c. sour cream
3 tbsp. butter
6 peppercorns
2 cloves garlic, chopped
salt to taste

Combine the water, vinegar, bay leaf and peppercorns. Pour this over the rabbit and refrigerate for several hours. Heat the butter in a saucepan. Drain the rabbit and add to the butter along with the onions, garlic and carrots. Season with salt. Saute the rabbit until well browned. Place the meat and vegetables in a greased casserole dish. Pour the sour cream into the butter that the rabbit cooked in and bring to a boil. Stir well and then pour over the rabbit and vegetables. Place the casserole dish in a moderate oven and bake at 350° for 45 minutes. Serves 4.

*

BIGOS
(Poland)

1 lb. pork, cubed
2 lb. sauerkraut

1 lb. Polish sausage, diced
1 c. mushrooms, sliced

¼ lb. bacon, diced
2 onions, sliced
2 cloves of garlic, minced
½ tsp. cumin
1 bay leaf

2 tsp. sugar
½ c. tomato puree
2 tsp. paprika
½ tsp. marjoram
2 c. white wine
salt and pepper to taste

Place the bacon and pork in a skillet and brown well. Add the onion and saute for five minutes. Add the sausage, sauerkraut, mushrooms, tomato puree, garlic, marjoram, sugar, paprika, cumin and bay leaf. Season with salt and pepper and move the bigos to a casserole dish. Add the white wine and enough water to cover. Cover the casserole dish, place in a moderate oven at 350° and bake for an hour and a half. Serves 6.

*

BOSANSKI LONAC—BOSNIAN CASSEROLE
(Croatia)

1 lb. beef, cubed
1 lb. pork or lamb, cubed
1 clove of garlic, chopped
1 onion, sliced
½ cabbage, shredded
5 potatoes, cubed

½ lb. green beans
2 sliced tomatoes
2 sliced green peppers
2 carrots, sliced
1 tbsp. parsley
¼ c. wine

Place the meat in the bottom of a large crock pot. Layer the vegetables over the meat. Season each layer with salt and pepper. Sprinkle the garlic and parsley over the vegetables. Leave the onion as the top layer. Add the wine and enough

*water or beef stock to cover. Cover the pot and allow to
simmer for several hours until both the meat and the
vegetables are tender. Serves 6.*

*

PORK KIDNEYS AND BARLEY
(Poland)

2 pork kidneys	1 c. barley
1 tbsp. flour	2 tbsp. butter
1 onion, finely chopped	¼ c. red wine
	salt to taste

*Slice the kidneys, place them in water and cook for fifteen to
twenty minutes. Remove from water and drain. Heat the
butter and brown the flour and chopped onion in it. Season
with salt. Add the kidneys and saute for about half an hour,
adding water as required. Cook the barley in 1½ cups of
salted water until tender. Add the cooked barley to the
kidneys. Pour in the red wine and cover. Allow to simmer for
another fifteen minutes. Serves 6.*

*

VEAL AND CUCUMBER CASSEROLE
(Bulgaria)

6 cucumbers, peeled	1 lb. veal, diced
1 onion, finely chopped	2 eggs, well beaten

2 tbsp. flour	salt and pepper to taste
2 tbsp. oil	dash of paprika

Heat the oil in a skillet and brown the meat in it. Add the onion and saute for five minutes. Slice the cucumbers lengthwise and coat with flour. Quickly fry the cucumbers in oil. Remove from the oil and place a layer of cucumbers in the bottom of a casserole dish. Add a layer of meat, then continue alternating cucumbers and meat. Season each layer with salt, pepper and paprika. Put the casserole in the oven and bake at 350° for half an hour. Remove from the oven and pour the beaten egg over the casserole. Return to the oven for another five minutes. Serves 4.

*

LOKSHNYA WITH HAM
(The Ukraine)

½ lb. ham, diced	2 c. flour
2 tbsp. water	2 tbsp. butter
1 egg, well beaten	3 tbsp. sour cream
1 tbsp. breadcrumbs	salt to taste

Place the flour on a board and make a well in the center. Combine the water and egg and place in the well. Work the flour into a dough and knead until it becomes elastic. Roll the dough out onto a floured board and let it sit for five minutes. Cut out 3/4 inch noodles and cook in salted boiling water for five minutes. Stir while the noodles cook. Heat the butter in a saucepan and brown the breadcrumbs in it. Drain the noodles and mix in the breadcrumbs and butter.

Combine the ham and sour cream and season with salt. Place a layer of noodles in a greased casserole dish and then a layer of ham. Continue layering until all the ingredients are used up. Bake the casserole in a hot oven at 450° for half an hour. Serves 4.

*

GHIVETCH—VEGETABLE CASSEROLE
(Bulgaria)

1 lb. potatoes, peeled
4 onions, sliced
1 lb. green peppers, sliced
1 carrot, sliced
2 c. yoghurt
dash of paprika

1 lb. tomatoes, peeled
and sliced
1 lb. green beans
2 c. oil
½ lb. eggplant, peeled
and cubed
salt and pepper to taste

Clean and cut the green beans. Prepare the remaining vegetables. Place the oil and vegetables in a pot and bring to a boil. Season with salt, pepper and paprika. Allow the vegetables to cook, covered, for about an hour, or until they become tender. Serve with yoghurt. Serves 4.

*

*

STUFFED PEPPERS
(Croatia)

1 lb. ground beef
1 c. rice
1 tbsp. chopped parsley
3 tbsp. flour
2 c. beef stock
1 c. sour cream

½ lb. smoked ham, diced
12 large green peppers
6 tbsp. oil
2 onions, chopped
¼ c. tomato paste
salt and pepper to taste

Brown the onion in 2 tbsp. oil. Add the meat and cook it in its own juices until the water has evaporated. Allow to cool slightly. Add the rice, salt, pepper and parsley and mix well. Wash the peppers, core them and remove the seeds and ribs. Stuff the peppers with the meat mixture. Do not stuff the peppers too full because the rice will expand while cooking. Arrange the peppers in a deep pot. Brown the flour in the remaining oil. Add the tomato paste and the beef stock. Stir well. Pour this sauce over the peppers. Add enough water to cover and simmer over low heat for approximately an hour and a half without mixing. Shake the pot occasionally so that the peppers do not stick. Carefully remove the peppers and arrange them in a warm serving dish. If desired, add sour cream to the tomato sauce. Cook for a few more minutes, then pour this sauce over the peppers. Serves 12 as an entree or 6 as a luncheon dish.

*

*

SAUERKRAUT AND SAUSAGE CASSEROLE
(Russia)

1½ c. sausage, diced	2 lb. sauerkraut
½ c. pickles, diced	3 tbsp. tomato puree
2 onions, finely chopped	1 tsp. sugar
1 tbsp. vinegar	1 bay leaf
1 tbsp. flour	1 tbsp. capers
3 tbsp. butter	½ c. beef stock
1 tbsp. parsley, chopped	salt and pepper to taste

Heat 2 tablespoons of butter in a saucepan. Add the sauerkraut and saute for ten minutes. Stir in the beef stock and cook, covered for half an hour. Add the tomato puree, vinegar, sugar, flour and bay leaf. Season with salt and pepper. Mix well and continue cooking for fifteen minutes. Heat the remaining butter in another saucepan. Add the onions, meat, pickles and capers. Saute the meat and onions for ten minutes. Grease a baking dish and place half the sauerkraut on the bottom. Lay the meat on the sauerkraut. Top with the other half of the sauerkraut. Sprinkle the parsley over the sauerkraut along with a little melted butter. Place the casserole in the oven and bake at 350° for fifteen minutes. Serves 4.

*

*

GOLUBTZI—STUFFED CABBAGE ROLLS
(The Ukraine)

2 lbs. ground beef
2 onions, finely chopped
½ c. sour cream
1 tbsp. flour

4 tbsp. cooked rice
4 tbsp. butter
2 c. beef stock
1 head of cabbage
salt and pepper to taste

Parboil the cabbage leaves in salted water for five to ten minutes. Allow the leaves to cool and then trim off the large ribs. Heat three tablespoons of butter in a saucepan and brown the onions and meat in it. Season with salt and pepper. Combine the meat, onions and rice. Place some of the meat filling on each cabbage leaf and roll it up, tucking in the top of the roll. Place the cabbage rolls in a greased baking dish. Heat the remaining tablespoon of butter in a saucepan. Add flour and stir in the beef stock and sour cream. Allow the sauce to cook over low heat for ten minutes, stirring constantly. Pour this sauce over the cabbage rolls and bake in a moderate oven at 350° for half an hour. In parts of the Ukraine and in Russia, tomato puree is added to the sauce. If this is desired, two tablespoons of tomato puree may be added to the sauce with the beef stock and sour cream. Serves 6.

*

*

STUFFED CABBAGE
(Czechoslovakia)

1 head of cabbage
1 onion, finely chopped
½ lb. ground beef
½ lb. sausage, diced
2 lb. sauerkraut
1 tsp. caraway seeds

2 tbsp. oil
1 tbsp. breadcrumbs
½ c. cooked rice
1 tbsp. sour cream
1½ c. beef stock
salt and pepper to taste

Parboil the head of cabbage in salted water for five to ten minutes. Cut out the inside of the cabbage head. Remove the outer leaves if the ribs are thick. Heat the oil in a saucepan and saute the beef, sausage, breadcrumbs, onion and half the caraway seeds for five to ten minutes in it. Season with salt and pepper. Remove from heat and mix in the sour cream and rice. Mix well. Stuff the head of cabbage with this mixture and place it in a greased baking dish. Tie the head, if necessary, to keep its shape. Place the sauerkraut in a saucepan with a little oil and the remaining caraway seeds. Cook the saurerkraut for 45 minutes. Place the sauerkraut around the cabbage. Pour the beef stock over the cabbage and sauerkraut. Cover the baking dish and bake in a moderate oven at 350° for one hour. Serve hot, topped with sour cream. Serves 6.

*

*

JELLIED PIG'S KNUCKLES
(The Ukraine)

2 lbs. pig's knuckles
1 carrot, sliced
1 onion, chopped
6 c. water

1 clove of garlic, minced
2 bay leaves
1 tbsp. parsley
4 hard-cooked eggs, sliced
salt and pepper to taste

Heat the water and add in the pig's knuckles. Cook for two to three hours until tender, removing the scum as it forms. When the knuckles have cooked for about an hour, add the vegetables, garlic, bay leaves and parsley. Season with salt and pepper. When the pig's knuckles are tender remove the meat from the bone and chop. Sprinkle a mold with paprika. Arrange the slices of hard-cooked eggs on the bottom of the mold. Add the meat back to the stock and pour the stock slowly over the egg slices. Refrigerate the jelly overnight. Serves 4-6. Jellied pork and other jellied meats are a traditional holiday dish among most Slavic people.

*

BANITZA
(Bulgaria)

Dough:

2 eggs
4 c. flour

3 tbsp. oil
1 c. warm water
½ tsp. salt

Filling:

1 lb. pot cheese or
   cottage cheese
2 eggs, well beaten
6 tbsp. Parmesan cheese

1/2 c. sour cream
1 tsp. salt
dash of pepper
6 tbsp. melted butter

Beat the eggs, salt, oil and warm water together. Add the flour and knead until a smooth dough is formed. If necessary, coat the hands with oil to keep the dough from sticking. Allow the dough to sit for two to three hours covered with clear wrap or a damp towel to keep it from drying out. Divide the dough into approximately eighteen balls. Roll each dough ball out onto a floured tablecloth and pull it with the fingers until it becomes paper thin. Combine the cheese and the eggs. Stir in the Parmesan cheese, sour cream, salt and pepper. Mix well. Grease a baking tin and place a sheet of dough in it. Coat the sheet with melted butter. Add more sheets until 6 or 7 have been used. Place a third of the filling on the dough, then add two more buttered sheets of dough and another third of the filling. Cover with two more sheets of buttered dough and the remaining filling. Cover with 6 or 7 more sheets of buttered dough. Coat the top with butter. Bake the Banitza in the oven at 350° for 30-40 minutes or until golden-brown. Serves 4.

*

BOSNIAN DJUVEDJE
(Croatia)

3 lbs. sliced tomatoes
2 zucchinis, sliced

1½ lbs. lamb, cubed
½ c. chopped green beans

2 tbsp. paprika
3 onions, sliced
1 c. green peppers, diced
½ c. white wine
1 eggplant, sliced

1 c. sliced cabbage
1 tbsp. chopped parsley
1 c. rice
½ c. shortening
salt and pepper to taste

Fry the rice in one tablespoon of shortening, but do not allow it to brown. When it becomes clear, add the rice to salted, boiling water and partially cook it. Drain. Heat the remaining shortening in a small saucepan and brown the onion in it. Season the meat with salt and pepper. Sprinkle with paprika. Grease a deep baking dish well. Line the bottom of the dish with the onion. Place a layer of tomatoes over the onion. Continue adding layers of vegetables until all are used up. Season each layer with salt and pepper. Leave the remaining tomatoes to form the top layers of the Djuvedje. *Sprinkle with parsley. Place the partially cooked rice over the vegetables. Arrange the seasoned meat on this bed of rice. Pour the wine over the casserole and bake at 350° until both the rice and the meat are tender. Serves 6.*

MEATS

MEATS

*

BEEF STROGANOFF
(Russia)

2 lbs. sirloin steak	1 c. mushrooms, sliced
1 onion, finely chopped	1 tsp. butter
1 c. sour cream	dash of nutmeg
	salt and pepper to taste

Slice the meat into thin strips about two inches long. This is best done when the meat is half frozen. Heat the butter in a saucepan and saute the onion and mushrooms in it until tender. Add the beef and season with nutmeg, salt and pepper. Allow the beef to cook for fifteen minutes. Slowly stir in the sour cream and mix well. Bring the Stroganoff to a quick boil and serve immediately in a heated serving dish. Serves 6.

*

ZAGREB VEAL CUTLETS
(Croatia)

6 large veal cutlets	2 eggs
6 thin slices smoked ham	½ c. fine breadcrumbs

6 thin slices Trappiste
    cheese
2 tbsp. milk
¼ c. flour

¼ c. butter
¼ c. oil
salt and pepper to taste

Trappiste cheese is not readily available everywhere. Port du Salut, a French version of the famous Croatian cheese makes a good substitute. Pound the veal cutlets with a meat tenderizer very well. Season with salt and pepper. Place a slice of cheese and a slice of ham on half of each cutlet. Fold the cutlet over and squeeze the edges firmly so that the filling does not show. Heat the oil and the butter together. Beat the eggs with the milk. Roll the cutlets in the flour. Dip them in the eggs. Roll each cutlet in breadcrumbs until it is well coated. Fry the cutlets on both sides over moderately high heat until they become on even golden color. Garnish with parsley and slices of lemon. Serves 6.

*

ROAST LAMB
(Bulgaria)

1 leg of lamb
4 cloves garlic
1 tbsp. wine vinegar

2 oz. olive oil
1 c. water
salt and pepper to taste

Slice the garlic cloves lengthwise and insert them into gashes in the leg of lamb. Place the leg of lamb in a roasting pan and season with salt and pepper. Combine the oil and vinegar and baste the meat with this mixture. Pour the water alongside the meat into the pan. Roast the leg of lamb in a

---

moderate oven at 350° for about three hours or until the meat is tender, basting frequently. Serves 6.

*

ROAST VEAL BREAST
(The Ukraine)

2 lbs. veal breast
2 lbs. cooked potatoes
2 tomatoes, sliced
¼ c. oil

¼ c. butter
2 onions, chopped
salt and pepper to taste

Season the meat and place in a roasting pan. Pour the oil over the veal breast and roast in a moderate oven at 350° until well roasted. Baste the meat frequently. Peel and cube the potatoes. Heat the butter in a saucepan and add the onions and potatoes. Season with salt and pepper. Saute the potatoes and onions until browned. Cut the veal breast into serving portions and place in a baking dish with the onions and potatoes. Arrange the tomato slices on top and cover with pan drippings. Place the meat and vegetables back in the oven and bake for an additional twenty minutes. Serves 6.

*

*

TEFTELI
(Russia)

1 lb. ground veal
1 onion, finely chopped
¼ c. flour
1 c. meat stock
1 tsp. garlic

2 c. breadcrumbs,
  soaked in milk
3 tbsp. oil
3 tbsp. tomato puree
1 bay leaf
salt and pepper to taste

Combine the ground veal, onion and breadcrumbs to form small meatballs. Roll the meatballs in flour and then brown in hot oil. Place the meatballs in a casserole dish and add the meat stock, tomato puree, bay leaf and garlic. Season with salt and pepper. Cover the dish and allow to bake in the oven at 350° for 20-25 minutes. Serves 4.

*

SVIČKOVA
(Czechoslovakia)

5 lbs. beef roast
2 onions, finely chopped
2 carrots, sliced
1 c. celery, diced
2 c. water
2 tbsp. flour
¾ c. sour cream

10 peppercorns
2 bay leaves
½ tsp. thyme
2 c. red wine
bacon for larding
3 cloves garlic, crushed
salt to taste

Lard the meat by placing bacon fat into gashes cut into the sides of the roast. Roll and tie the roast. Combine the onions, carrots, celery, red wine, water, peppercorns, bay leaves, thyme and garlic. Season with salt. Pour this marinade over the meat and marinate overnight. Place the meat and marinade into a baking dish and bake at 350° for 2-2½ hours. Baste frequently. Strain the juices that the meat has cooked in and place in a saucepan. Add the flour and cook over low heat, stirring constantly to form a roux. Stir in the sour cream and cook over low heat for a minute or two. Pour the sour cream sauce over the roast and serve. Serves 8-10.

✳

PRUNES AND VEAL
(Bulgaria)

2 lb. veal, cubed
2 c. prunes, pitted
4 tbsp. olive oil

½ tsp. cloves, crushed
¼ tsp. sugar
1 onion, chopped
salt and pepper to taste

Finely chop the prunes. Heat the olive oil in a saucepan and saute the prunes for 5 minutes. Remove the prunes and quickly brown the veal and onion. Add the prunes and the remaining ingredients and season with salt and pepper. Cover the pan and cook for one hour or until the meat is tender. Shake the pan occasionally to prevent sticking. Serves 6.

✳

*

BREADED TONGUE CUTLETS
(Poland)

2 lbs. ox tongue
1 c. breadcrumbs
¼ c. flour

2 eggs, well beaten
4 tbsp. butter
salt and pepper to taste

Wash the tongue, place in salted water and cook until tender. When tender, drain and remove the skin. Slice the tongue into cutlets. Season the cutlets with salt and pepper, roll in the flour, dip in the beaten egg and then roll in the breadcrumbs. Heat the butter in a skillet so that it is hot and quickly fry the cutlets until golden brown. Serves 6.

*

PORK CHOPS WITH APPLES
(Czechoslovakia)

2 lbs. pork chops
1 onion, finely chopped
2 tbsp. oil

4 apples
¾ c. water
salt to taste

Peel and slice the apples. Season the pork chops with salt. Heat the oil in a skillet and brown the pork. Add the onion and saute with the pork for five minutes. Add the sliced apples and water. Cover the pork chops and allow to cook slowly for about twenty minutes. Serves 6.

*

PORK COOKED IN BEER
(Russia)

4 lbs. pork butt
1 c. bacon, diced

2 c. beer
salt and pepper to taste

Fry the bacon in a skillet to render the fat. Clean the leg of pork and place in a roasting pan. Season the meat with salt and pepper. Cut the skin open on the leg of pork. Pour the bacon and bacon fat over the meat. Roast the leg in the oven at 375°. Pour one cup of beer over the pork when it is first placed in the oven. Baste with the remaining beer, as required, while the pork is roasting. Serves 6-8.

*

PAPRIKA VEAL
(Czechoslavakia)

2 lbs. veal, cubed
½ c. bacon, diced
 half an onion, chopped
¼ c. water

¼ c. tomato paste
1 tsp. paprika
1 c. sour cream
salt and pepper to taste

Fry the bacon in its own fat for five to ten minutes. Add the veal and onion. Fry for another five minutes. Add the water and tomato paste and season with paprika, salt and pepper. Allow the veal to cook slowly in this sauce for half an hour. Stir in the sour cream and simmer for another five minutes. Serves 6.

*

PORK AND VEGETABLES
(Poland)

2 lb. pork, cubed
1 red cabbage, shredded
3 parsnips, cubed
2 tbsp. oil

4 carrots, sliced
1 onion, finely chopped
2 cloves garlic, minced
salt and pepper to taste

Heat the oil in a large saucepan and add the garlic and pork. Brown the meat well. Add the vegetables. Season with salt and pepper. Pour in ½ cup water and allow to cook, covered for an hour, or until the vegetables are cooked and the meat is tender. Serves 6.

*

VEAL PATTIES WITH SOUR CREAM
(Poland)

2 lb. ground veal
1 onion, finely chopped
1 c. sour cream
½ c. breadcrumbs

2 tbsp. oil
2 eggs, well beaten
2 cloves garlic, minced
salt and pepper to taste

Combine the meat, breadcrumbs, eggs, garlic and onion. Season with salt and pepper and mix well. Make 3 inch patties from the meat. Heat the oil in a pan and brown the patties in the oil. Pour the sour cream over the patties. Cover the pan and cook slowly for 20 minutes. Serves 6.

*

BEEF RIBS WITH KOHLRABI
(Czechoslovakia)

3 lbs. beef short ribs
1 tbsp. butter
2 c. meat stock

1 lb. kohlrabi, diced
1 tbsp. flour
½ tsp. sugar
salt and pepper to taste

Cut the ribs into serving portions. Place the meat in a saucepan and season with salt and pepper. Cover with meat stock. Simmer slowly for about an hour. Add the kohlrabi and cook for an additional hour. Add water if necessary. Heat the butter in another pan and stir the flour and sugar. Season with salt and pepper. Brown the flour to make a thick roux. Add the roux to the meat and kohlrabi. Allow the sauce to thicken and serve. Serves 6.

*

PAŠTICADA—DALMATIAN POT ROAST
(Croatia)

2 lb. beef roast
6 cloves
4 cloves garlic, slivered
2 oz. bacon slices
1 onion, finely chopped

1 c. red table wine
1 tbsp. tomato paste
1¼ c. beef stock
¼ c. lard
salt and pepper to taste

Wash the roast, wipe it with a kitchen towel and lard it with bacon. Make small slits in the side of the roast and insert the garlic and clove in them. Season with salt and pepper and refrigerate overnight. The following day, brown the meat on all sides in the well heated lard. Add the onion and simmer slowly until the meat soaks up all the juices. Add the wine and tomato paste. Cook for approximately twenty minutes. Add the beef stock and simmer slowly for approximately two hours. If necessary, add a little water occasionally. Remove the roast, slice thinly and place on a serving platter. Strain the gravy and cook it for another half hour. If required, thicken the gravy with a little flour browned in hot fat. Pour this sauce over the sliced roast before serving. Serves 6.

*

STEWED CALF'S HEART
(Slovenia)

2 calf's hearts	2 tbsp. butter
1 onion, finely chopped	2 tbsp. flour
¼ c. carrots, sliced	4 peppercorns
1 bay leaf	salt to taste

Wash the hearts and remove the veins and arteries. Cook the hearts in salted boiling water for one and half hours. Cut into smaller pieces and remove fat and any remaining veins and arteries. Place the hearts in a saucepan and add the carrots, onion, peppercorns and bay leaf. Pour in one cup of water and season with salt. Allow to cook slowly for fifteen minutes. Heat the butter in a saucepan and brown the flour in it. Add the flour and butter to the hearts and cook for five to ten minutes until a medium sauce forms. Serves 4.

LIVER IN SOUR CREAM
(Russia)

2 lbs. beef liver, sliced
2 onions, finely chopped
1 c. sour cream
2 c. water

¼ c. butter
2 tbsp. flour
1 tbsp. chopped parsley
salt and pepper to taste

Season the liver with salt and pepper. Dredge in flour. Heat the butter in a saucepan and saute the liver in it for five minutes. Add the onions and saute until tender. Stir in the water and sour cream and mix well. Cover the meat and allow to cook slowly for 45 minutes. Serve with the sour cream sauce and sprinkled with the parsley. Serve 6.

*

BOSNIAN LAMB PILAV
(Croatia)

2 lbs. shoulder of lamb, cubed
¼ c. lard or shortening
¼ c. butter
1½ c. rice

¼ c. tomato paste
1 c. onion, finely chopped
1 clove garlic, crushed
2 c. water
salt and pepper to taste

Saute the finely chopped onion in the lard until golden brown. Add the crushed garlic and stir well. Brown the cubed meat in the lard. Season with salt and pepper. Cover and simmer slowly for about fifteen minutes, stirring frequently. Add the tomato paste and a little water. Allow to simmer for approximately half an hour, stirring occasionally. If necessary, add just a little water. Wash the rice and saute it in the hot butter, but do not allow it to brown. When the rice becomes clear, add two cups of water, cover and cook slowly until tender. Place the rice on a large serving platter. Arrange the lamb in the center and serve immediately. Serves 6.

*

PIG'S KNUCKLES WITH SAUERKRAUT
(The Ukraine)

4 pig's knuckles
4 c. sauerkraut
1 c. bacon, diced

8 c. boiling water
salt and pepper to taste

Place the pig's knuckles in the boiling water and cook for two to three hours. Fry the bacon in a saucepan until crisp. Drain the sauerkraut and add to the bacon. Add the pig's knuckles and season with salt and pepper. Cook for 45 minutes over medium heat or until the meat is so tender that it almost falls off the bones. Serves 4.

*

*

BRAISED OXTAIL
(Czechoslovakia)

1 oxtail, cut into pieces
2 onions, finely chopped
2 tbsp. celery, diced
1 tomato, chopped
1 parnsip, cubed
3 tbsp. oil

2 tbsp. flour
1 carrot, sliced
1 c. hot water
2 bay leaves
½ tsp. cloves
salt and pepper to taste

Heat the oil in a saucepan and brown the oxtail. Add the carrot, onions, celery and parsnip. Season with salt and pepper. Saute the vegetables until well browned. Sprinkle in the flour and allow it to brown. Slowly, stir in the water. Add the chopped tomato, bay leaves and cloves. Cook the oxtail over low heat for 30 minutes or until the meat is tender. Serves 4.

*

BEEF KOTLETY
(Russia)

2 lbs. ground beef
2 onions, finely chopped
½ c. breadcrumbs
1 c. milk

4 slices bread
2 eggs, well beaten
¼ c. sour cream
salt and pepper to taste

Soak the bread in the milk. Drain the bread and mix well with the ground beef. Add the onions and eggs and mix well. Season with salt and pepper. Shape the meat into patties 4 inches wide and coat with breadcrumbs. Heat the butter in a skillet and fry the patties in the butter until brown. Remove to a heated platter. Add the sour cream to the butter and cook for five minutes, stirring constantly. Pour the sour cream over the kotlety and serve. Serves 6.

*

PORK ROAST
(Czechoslavakia)

4 lb. pork roast   4 tbsp. caraway seeds
1½ c. water   salt and pepper to taste

Season the roast with salt and pepper. Place the meat in a greased roasting pan. Sprinkle the caraway seeds on the roast and alongside the meat. Pour in the water. Roast the meat in a moderate oven at 350° for two to three hours. Baste the meat frequently, adding water as required. Serves 8.

*

*

ROAST SUCKLING PIG
(Croatia)

1 suckling pig
¼ c. lard or oil

2 oz. smoked bacon, sliced
1 c. beer
salt to taste

Clean and wash the suckling pig well. Dry it inside and out with a kitchen towel. Season the piglet very well with salt. Refrigerate for several hours or overnight. The following day, wipe the piglet with a kitchen towel to remove any excess salt. This will prevent the skin from blistering while roasting. Place an empty bottle in the stomach cavity and sew up the edges. This will help the roast to maintain its shape. Place the piglet on a metal rack in a large roasting pan. Pour hot oil over the roast. Place it in a warm oven and roast at 325° for about 45 minutes for every pound of weight. Baste frequently with the smoked bacon slices which have been dipped in beer. If the ears and tail begin to brown too soon, wrap them in aluminum foil so that they will not become overly crisp. When the roast is an even golden brown, remove from the oven. Allow to cool for about five minutes. Remove the bottle from the cavity. Place an apple in the pig's mouth and serve whole. Serves 8.

*

*

PORK IN WINE
(Bulgaria)

2 lbs. pork, cubed	1 c. white wine
2 tbsp. flour	2 cloves garlic, minced
1 bay leaf	1 c. water
1 tbsp. olive oil	salt and pepper to taste

Heat the olive oil in a saucepan. Add the pork cubes and cook for half an hour, covered. Slowly pour in the wine and water. Add the bay leaf and garlic. Season with salt and pepper. Allow the meat to cook another half an hour or until tender. Combine some of the liquid that the meat has cooked in with the flour. Add the flour and water to the meat and cook for five minutes until a medium sauce forms. Serves 6.

*

LAMB AND CABBAGE STEW
(Russia)

2 lbs. lamb, cubed	2 tbsp. butter
1 c. sauerkraut	1 bay leaf
1 head of cabbage	1 c. water
1 onion, finely chopped	salt and pepper to taste

Heat the butter in a saucepan and brown the lamb in it. Shred the cabbage. Remove the meat and replace with the cabbage and onion. Season with salt and pepper. Saute the cabbage and onion for ten minutes. Add the sauerkraut, bay leaf and the water. Add the meat and season once more. Cover the pan and allow to simmer slowly for an hour or until meat is tender. Serves 6.

*

MUTTON AND VEGETABLES
(Czechoslovakia)

2 lbs. mutton, cubed	2 cloves garlic, minced
½ c. celery, diced	2 carrots, sliced
1 onion, finely chopped	2 parsnips, cubed
¼ c. butter	½ tsp. marjoram
2 c. water	2 tbsp. flour
	salt and pepper to taste

Heat the butter in a saucepan and brown the meat in it with the garlic. Add the vegetables and saute for five to ten minutes. Season with salt and pepper. Add the marjoram and water. Allow the meat and vegetables to cook slowly for two hours. When the meat is done add the flour and bring to a boil. Cook for another five minutes. Serves 6.

*

*

SAUSAGE AND RED CABBAGE
(Poland)

1 lb. sausage, sliced	1 tbsp. flour
1 head red cabbage	2 tbsp. wine vinegar
2 tbsp. butter	½ c. red wine
1 tsp. worchestershire	½ tsp. sugar
sauce	salt and pepper to taste

Shred the cabbage into strips and boil in salted water for a minute or two. Drain the cabbage. Melt the butter in a saucepan and stir in the wine and flour. Add the wine vinegar, sugar, cabbage and worchestershire sauce. Season with salt and pepper. Cook the cabbage for twenty minutes. Add the sausage and cook for another ten to fifteen minutes. Serves 4.

*

LAMB CHOPS WITH PRUNES
(The Ukraine)

6 lamb chops	2 tsp. sugar
1 onion, finely chopped	1 cloves
1 c. prunes, diced	1 tbsp. vinegar
1 tbsp. tomato puree	1 tbsp. flour
2 c. water	2 tbsp. butter
	salt and pepper to taste

Soak the prunes in milk overnight. Heat the butter in a saucepan and add in the lamb chops. Season with salt and pepper. Saute the lamb chops until browned. Remove the lamb chops and brown the onion. Add the lambchops, tomato puree and water. Cover and allow to cook for five to ten minutes. Add the prunes, sugar, vinegar and cloves. Allow to cook for another half hour. Remove the lamb chops and prunes and place on a serving platter. Strain the liquid in which the lamb was cooked. Add the flour to the liquid and cook until it thickens. Pour this sauce over the lamb chops and serve. Serves 6.

*

SIRLOIN STEAK À LA BAČKA
(Croatia)

6 sirloin steaks
¼ c. flour
¼ c. shortening
1 c. onions, sliced
½ c. smoked bacon,
   sliced into 1" strips
1 tsp. paprika

2 green peppers
2 firm ripe tomatoes
1 tbsp. tomato paste
½ c. mushrooms, sliced
2 tsp. minced garlic
pinch marjoram
salt and pepper to taste

Season the flour with salt and pepper. Roll the steaks in the seasoned flour. Brown them in hot shortening, then place them in a large saucepan. Saute the onions in the shortening until they become golden brown. Add the paprika, tomato paste, garlic and marjoram. Stir well. Cook this sauce for a few minutes. Add the sauce to the steaks. If necessary, add water or beef stock to cover. Cover the saucepan and simmer over low heat until the meat is nearly tender, adding water as required. Turn the steaks occasionally. Fry the bacon in its own fat, but do not crisp. Add the mushrooms, peeled and sliced tomatoes and sliced green peppers. Season with salt and pepper and simmer, covered, for about ten to fifteen minutes. Add this vegetable sauce to the steaks and continue cooking slowly until both the vegetables and the steaks are tender. Serves 6.

*

SHASHLIK
(Russia)

1 lb. lamb
¼ c. olive oil
2 cloves garlic, crushed
1 tsp. paprika

1 lb. pork
juice 2 lemons
6 small onions
salt and pepper to taste

Combine the olive oil, lemon juice, garlic, paprika and salt and pepper. Mix well. Cube the meat and place it in the marinade. Refrigerate overnight. The following day, quarter the onions. Alternate meat cubes and onion sections on skewers. Brush with olive oil. Grill over coals until the meat is well browned on the outside and tender on the inside. Serves 6.

SAUCES

SAUCES

*

LIVER SAUCE
(Czechoslovakia)

2 c. liver, finely chopped
2 c. beef stock or water
¼ tsp. caraway seeds
dash of marjoram

1 onion, finely chopped
¼ c. flour
3 tbsp. oil
salt and pepper to taste

Heat the oil in a skillet and saute the onion. Add the flour and liver and sautee until golden brown. Season with marjoram, salt and pepper. Stir in the beef stock and caraway seeds. Allow the sauce to simmer until thickened.

*

WINE GRAVY
(Croatia)

½ c. beef roast pan
  drippings
¼ c. flour

½ c. red wine
1½ c. beef stock
salt and pepper to taste

Heat the pan drippings. Stir in the flour and cook over medium heat for a few minutes. Add the beef stock slowly, stirring constantly so that lumps do not form. Stir in the wine. Season with salt and pepper. Cook until the sauce thickens. Serve with roast beef or lamb.

*

TOMATO SAUCE
(Czechoslovakia)

1 onion, finely chopped	½ lb. tomatoes
1 c. water	¼ c. flour
1 c. sour cream	salt to taste
2 tbsp. butter	

Peel and chop the tomatoes. Heat the butter in a skillet and saute the onion in it until soft. Add the tomatoes and water. Season with salt and cook for fifteen minutes. Put the sauce through a sieve. Stir in the flour slowly to avoid lumps and then add the sour cream. Bring the sauce to a quick boil and then serve.

*

BEET SAUCE
(The Ukraine)

4 beets, peeled	2 tbsp. horseradish
1 onion, finely chopped	wine vinegar
	salt to taste

Place the beets in water and boil until tender. Remove the beets and grate. Combine the grated beets with the chopped onion and prepared horseradish. Season with salt and mix well. Cover the beets with wine vinegar and refrigerate. This is an excellent sauce to serve with cold meats in summer.

✳

CAPER SAUCE
(Slovenia)

2 tbsp. capers
1½ c. beef stock
2 tbsp. flour

2 tbsp. butter
salt and pepper to taste

Heat the butter in a saucepan and blend in the flour. Allow to turn golden, stirring constantly. Pour in the beef stock slowly, while stirring. Bring the sauce to a boil and add in the capers and simmer for another five minutes or until the sauce thickens. Season with salt and pepper. Caper sauce is excellent with boiled fish.

✳

POLISH SAUCE
(Poland)

¼ c. raisins
1 onion, finely chopped

¼ c. almonds,
    blanched and sliced

2 tbsp. butter   4 tbsp. flour
2 tbsp. prunes, chopped   1½ c. beef stock
1 tbsp. currant jam   ¼ c. red wine
                              salt to taste

Cook the prunes in ¼ cup of water. When well cooked, drain and finely mash. Heat the butter in a saucepan and saute the onion in it. Add the flour and saute until a roux forms. Add the beef stock to the roux and simmer for fifteen minutes. Add the remaining ingredients and season with salt. Simmer the sauce for another fifteen to twenty minutes. Serve with beef.

*

SOUR CREAM SAUCE
(Russia)

1 c. sour cream   2 tbsp. butter
2 tbsp. flour   2 c. beef stock
1 onion, finely chopped   salt and pepper to taste

Heat the butter in a skillet and saute the onion in it. Add the flour and allow to turn golden, forming a roux. Stir constantly. Stir in the beef stock and bring to a boil. Season with salt and pepper. Allow the sauce to cool, then blend in the sour cream. Reheat the sauce slowly until thickened.

*

*

MAYONNAISE WITH WINE
(Poland)

5 egg yolks
½ c. white wine
juice of one lemon

1 c. oil
1 tsp. sugar
1 envelope gelatin
salt and pepper to taste

Dissolve the gelatin in the wine. Stir in the olive oil and lemon juice. Blend in the sugar and season with salt and pepper. Beat the mayonnaise and add the egg yolks. Continue beating until the mayonnaise thickens. Serve the sauce with boiled fish.

*

DILL SAUCE
(Slovenia)

2 tbsp. dill
2 c. beef stock

2 tbsp. butter
2 tbsp. flour
salt to taste

Heat the butter in a saucepan and stir in the flour slowly. Allow the flour to turn golden and form a roux. Pour in the beef stock slowly and bring to a boil. Season with salt. Add the dill and simmer for another five minutes or until the sauce thickens.

*

MUSTARD SAUCE
(The Ukraine)

2 tbsp. mustard	3 tbsp. butter
1 onion, finely chopped	2 tbsp. flour
½ c. white wine	1 c. beef or chicken stock
dash Worcestershire sauce	

Heat the butter in a saucepan and saute the onion until golden. Stir in the flour and allow to form a roux. Add the stock and wine. Bring the sauce to a boil and simmer for two to three minutes. Add the mustard and Worcestershire sauce and simmer for another minute or two. Serve this sauce with sausage, ham or pork.

*

HORSERADISH SAUCE WITH CREAM
(Poland)

¾ c. fresh horseradish	juice of 1/2 a lemon
¾ c. cream	1½ tsp. sugar

Grate the horseradish and allow to stand for an hour or two. Stir the horseradish into the cream and mix well. Add the sugar and lemon juice. Blend thoroughly and serve with boiled fish.

*

*

WALNUT SAUCE
(Bulgaria)

½ c. walnuts, ground
2 tbsp. olive oil
1 tbsp. garlic, minced

1 slice white bread
½ c. milk
juice of 1/2 lemon
salt and pepper to taste

Combine the walnuts and garlic and mix well. Soak the bread in the milk and drain. Squeeze out the remaining milk and mix the bread with the walnuts. Blend the mixture until smooth. Add the olive oil slowly with the lemon juice, mixing the walnuts into a paste. Thin the paste into a smooth thick sauce with milk or water. Season the sauce with salt and pepper and mix once again. Serve with grilled meat or poultry.

*

OLIVE SAUCE
(Croatia)

12 pitted green olives
2 tbsp. olive oil
5 anchovy fillets

3 c. clear stock
2 tbsp. flour
salt and pepper to taste

Heat the olive oil over medium heat. Add the flour and allow it to brown, stirring constantly. Slowly stir in the stock and bring the mixture to a boil. Continue stirring. Lower the heat and allow the sauce to cook for a few minutes. Finely chop the olives and the anchovy fillets. Add them to the sauce. Season the sauce with salt and pepper. This tangy sauce is excellent with lamb. It can also be served with grilled or baked fish dishes.

*

PICKLE SAUCE
(Poland)

½ c. pickles, chopped
1 c. beef stock
1 tsp. sugar
2 tbsp. butter

½ c. pickle juice
¾ c. sour cream
1 tbsp. flour
salt to taste

Heat the beef stock and cook the pickles in it for two to three minutes. Heat the butter in a saucepan and brown the flour in it to form a roux. Slowly add the stock and pickles to the roux. Stir in the sour cream, pickle juice, sugar and salt. Allow to simmer another two to three minutes and serve. This is an excellent fish sauce.

*

*

MUSHROOM SAUCE
(Russia)

½ c. mushrooms, finely
  chopped
1 c. sour cream
1 tsp. Worcestershire sauce

1 onion, finely chopped
1 tbsp. flour
½ c. beef stock
2 tbsp. butter

Heat the butter in a saucepan and saute the mushrooms and onion in it until soft. Stir in the flour and allow to brown. Slowly pour in the beef stock and simmer for two to three minutes. Stir in the sour cream and Worcestershire sauce and bring to a boil. This sauce can be served with vegetables and most meats.

*

CARAWAY SAUCE
(Czechoslovakia)

½ tsp. caraway seeds
2 tbsp. butter
1 clove of garlic, minced
2 tbsp. flour

2 c. beef or chicken stock
1 tsp. parsley
salt and pepper to taste

Heat the butter in a saucepan and brown the flour in it. Add the caraway seeds, parsley and garlic. Slowly pour in the meat stock, stirring constantly. Season with salt and pepper. Allow the sauce to simmer for half an hour.

*

CHIVE SAUCE
(Poland)

2 tbsp. chives, finely
  chopped
¾ c. sour cream
1 tbsp. lemon juice

1¼ c. beef or chicken stock
2 tbsp. butter
2 tbsp. flour
salt and pepper to taste

Heat the butter in a saucepan and blend in the flour. Allow the flour to brown and form a roux, stirring constantly. Pour in the meat stock slowly, and continue stirring the sauce. Add the lemon juice, chives and season the sauce with salt and pepper. Allow the sauce to simmer for two to three minutes. Blend in the sour cream and bring the sauce to a boil. Serve this sauce hot with meats.

*

PAPRIKA SAUCE
(Slovenia)

½ tbsp. paprika
2 tbsp. sour cream
1 tbsp. flour

1 onion, finely chopped
2 c. beef or chicken stock
2 tbsp. butter
salt to taste

Melt the butter in a saucepan and saute the onion until golden. Add the flour and allow to brown to form a roux.

Slowly, add the meat stock, stirring constantly. Season the sauce with salt. Add the paprika and allow to simmer for five minutes. Stir in the sour cream and bring to a boil. Serve with meat and poultry dishes.

*

YOGHURT SAUCE
(Bulgaria)

2 c. yoghurt	½ c. beef or chicken stock
2 cloves of garlic, minced	1 tbsp. butter
1 tbsp. chopped parsley	2 tbsp. flour
1 tbsp. dill, finely chopped	½ tsp. paprika
	salt and pepper to taste

Heat the butter in a saucepan. Add the garlic and saute for a minute or two. Add the flour and yoghurt, stirring constantly. Add the paprika, dill and parsley. Season the sauce with salt and pepper. Add the meat stock and cook the sauce for a minute or two. Serve with fish or boiled vegetables.

*

GRILLED MEAT SAUCE
(Croatia)

1 c. currant jelly	2 onions
	½ c. Dijon-type mustard

Finely chop the onion. Mix all the ingredients and heat to just below the boiling point. Serve with cevapcici or other grilled meats.

*

GARLIC SAUCE
(Croatia)

3 tbsp. shortening
3 tbsp. flour
½ c. sour cream

5-6 cloves garlic or
  5-6 tsp. powdered garlic
1 c. beef stock
salt and pepper to taste

Mix the salt and pepper with the garlic. Heat the shortening over medium heat and stir in the flour. When the flour begins to brown, stir in the garlic slowly, mixing well so that lumps do not form. Mince the garlic if you are using whole cloves. Dilute the roux with the beef stock. Allow to cook for about a minute or two. Add the sour cream and bring the sauce to a boil, stirring constantly until creamy. Remove from heat and serve immediately. This sauce is excellent with pork, lamb or fish, but may also be served with cooked vegetables.

SALADS

SALADS

*

ZAGREB SALAD
(Croatia)

2 small tomatoes
1 head lettuce
1 tbsp. chopped parsley,
½ c. fresh mushrooms,
  sliced
1 cucumber, peeled

1 green pepper
4 stalks green onion
¼ c. sliced radishes
2 tbsp. vinegar
¼ c. smoked bacon, diced
salt and pepper to taste

Clean and wash the vegetables. Slice the tomatoes. Chop the green pepper and green onion. Slice the radishes, mushrooms and cucumber. Place the vegetables in a bowl and season with salt, pepper and parsley. Fry the bacon in its own fat. Add the vinegar to the bacon, but do not remove from heat. When the mixture begins to boil, remove from heat, pour over the salad, toss well and serve immediately.

*

KOHLRABI SALAD
(Czechoslovakia)

6 kohlrabi
1 tbsp. oil

½ c. water
2 tbsp. vinegar

157

½ tsp. sugar
dash of paprika

1 clove garlic, diced
salt and pepper to taste

Peel and grate the kohlrabi. Try to use young kohlrabi as they are tender. Combine the remaining ingredients to make a dressing. Pour the dressing over the kohlrabi and mix well.

*

CELERY ROOT AND POTATO SALAD
(Poland)

2 celery roots
2 potatoes
1 tbsp. chopped chives

¼ c. oil
2 tbsp. wine vinegar
1 tbsp. dill, chopped

Scrape celery roots and peel the potatoes. Cook in boiling water until tender. Drain. Slice the potatoes and celery root and place in a bowl. Combine the remaining ingredients to make a dressing. Pour the dressing over the salad and serve.

*

MIXED SALAD
(Bulgaria)

2 cucumbers
1 tomato, sliced

1 onion, thinly sliced
1 green pepper, sliced

¼ c. black olives, chopped
2 tbsp. vinegar
¼ tsp. paprika

5 tbsp. olive oil
2 cloves garlic, diced
salt and pepper to taste

Peel the cucumbers and slice lengthwise. Hold the two halves together and cut into slices. Salt the cucumbers and allow them to sit for half an hour. Also salt the onion and allow it to sit. Combine the oil, vinegar, garlic and paprika. Season with salt and pepper. Drain the cucumbers and place in a bowl with the onions, green pepper and olives. Pour the two-thirds of the dressing over the salad and toss. Place the tomato slices on top of the salad and pour the remaining dressing over the tomato slices.

*

CAULIFLOWER SALAD
(Czechoslovakia)

1 head cauliflower
½ c. water
1 tsp. sugar
dash of paprika
6 peppercorns

3 tbsp. vinegar
3 tbsp. oil
1 clove garlic, diced
1 bay leaf
salt and pepper to taste

Break the cauliflower into flowerets and cook in salted water with the bay leaf and peppercorns until tender. Combine the remaining ingredients to make a dressing. Pour the dressing over the cauliflower and chill.

*

*

ZUCCHINI SALAD
(Bulgaria)

4 medium zucchinis
2 carrots
½ tbsp. dill, chopped

3 tbsp. olive oil
2 tbsp. vinegar
½ tbsp. parsley, chopped
salt and pepper to taste

Grate the zucchinis and carrots. Combine them and season with parsley and dill. Combine the oil, vinegar, salt and pepper. Pour this dressing over the vegetables and serve. Serves 4.

*

RUSSIAN SALAD WITH MAYONNAISE
(Russia)

3 c. cooked potatoes, diced
2 c. ham, diced
1 c. pickles, diced
2 egg yolks, well beaten
2 c. oil

1 tbsp. capers, crushed
1 c. peas
¼ tsp. paprika
3 tbsp. vinegar
1 tsp. mustard
salt and pepper to taste

Combine the potatoes, ham, capers, peas, and pickles. Mix together in a separate bowl the egg yolks, paprika, mustard and vinegar. Slowly add the oil, a little at a time, beating the mixture vigorously with each addition. Season with salt and pepper. If the mayonnaise starts to curdle, add a third egg yolk and a small bit of oil. This should stop the curdling. Mix the mayonnaise into the ham and potato mixture. Chill the salad for two hours and then serve.

*

VEAL SALAD WITH MAYONNAISE
(Czechoslovakia)

1 c. veal, diced
1 onion, finely chopped
1 c. pickles, diced
¼ tsp. paprika
2 tbsp. vinegar

1 c. apples, diced
1 c. cooked pork, diced
2 egg yolks, well beaten
¼ tsp. mustard
1 c. oil

Combine the veal, pork, pickles, onion and apples. Mix together in a separate bowl the egg yolks, paprika, mustard and vinegar. Slowly add the oil, beating vigorously with each addition. Season with salt and pepper. If the mayonnaise begins to curdle, add a third egg yolk and a small bit of oil. This should stop the curdling. Stir the mayonnaise into the veal and apple mixture and mix well. Chill the salad for two hours and then serve.

*

*

WILTED LETTUCE SALAD
(Russia)

1 head of Bibb lettuce   2 tbsp. vinegar
½ tsp. sugar   1 c. bacon, diced

Fry the bacon until crisp. Drain the fat and combine it with the vinegar and sugar. Allow to cook for a minute or two. Sprinkle the lettuce with the bacon.. Pour the hot fat over the lettuce and mix well.

*

EGG AND LETTUCE SALAD
(Poland)

1 head of lettuce   2 hard-cooked egg yolks
1 tsp. sugar   1 tbsp. vinegar
1 c. sour cream   salt to taste

Chop the egg yolks. Combine them with the sugar, vinegar and sour cream. Season with salt. Tear the lettuce into bite-sized chunks. Pour the dressing over the lettuce and serve.

*

*

CROATIAN CUCUMBERS
(Croatia)

4 large cucumbers   ¾ c. sour cream
1 tsp. minced garlic   salt and pepper to taste

Wash the cucumbers and peel them. Slice the whole cucumbers down the center. Keeping the two halves together, slice as thinly as desired. Season with salt and pepper and refrigerate for at least an hour. Drain. Pour the sour cream over the drained cucumbers. Add the garlic. Mix well. If desired, sprinkle with a little paprika.

*

SAUERKRAUT SALAD
(Poland)

1 lb. sauerkraut   1 apple, diced
2 tbsp. olive oil   1 tsp. sugar
    salt and pepper to taste

Combine the apple and the sauerkraut. Add the oil. Sprinkle with sugar and season the sauerkraut with salt and pepper. Mix well before serving.

*

*

RED CABBAGE SALAD
(The Ukraine)

1 head red cabbage	4 tbsp. salad oil
2 tbsp. vinegar	2 tsp. sugar
½ c. red peppers, chopped	salt and pepper to taste

Coarsley chop the cabbage and boil in salted water for a minute. Drain and place in a bowl with the red peppers. Combine the remaining ingredients to make a dressing. Mix well and pour over the cabbage.

*

CABBAGE SALAD
(Poland)

1 head cabbage, chopped	4 tbsp. salad oil
1 onion, finely chopped	2 tbsp. vinegar
2 tbsp. parsley	1 clove garlic, diced
1 tsp. sugar	salt and pepper to taste

Combine the cabbage and onion and season with salt and pepper. Allow to sit for half an hour. Combine the remaining ingredients to make a dressing. Mix well. Pour the dressing over the cabbage and serve.

*

*

VEGETABLE SALAD
(The Ukraine)

½ c. cooked carrots, sliced
½ c. cooked peas
½ c. celery, diced
½ c. cooked beets, diced
1 tomato, chopped
1 small red pepper, diced
1 c. salad oil
½ tbsp. mustard

1 apple, diced
¼ c. green onions, finely
  chopped
½ c. sour cream
2 uncooked egg yolks
2 tbsp. vinegar
2 hard-cooked eggs
¼ tsp. paprika
salt and pepper to taste

Chop the hard-cooked eggs. Combine all the vegetables, apple and hard-cooked eggs. Season with salt and pepper. Combine the well beaten egg yolks, paprika, and vinegar. Slowly add small amounts of oil, beating vigorously with each addition. The mayonnaise should be thick and creamy. Blend in the mustard and sour cream. Add the dressing to the vegetables and mix well. Chill for an hour or two before serving.

*

GREEN SALAD WITH YOGHURT DRESSING
(Slovenia)

1 head of lettuce
½ tsp. sugar

3 stalks green onion
dash of paprika

¼ c. yoghurt   1 tbsp. olive oil
                                salt and pepper to taste

Shred the lettuce and chop the green onion. Place the lettuce and green onion in a bowl. Combine the yoghurt, olive oil, sugar and paprika. Season with salt and pepper. Pour the dressing over the lettuce and toss.

*

TOMATO SALAD
(Bulgaria)

2 lbs. tomatoes, sliced   3 tbsp. olive oil
2 onions, sliced   1 tbsp. vinegar
1 tbsp. water   salt and pepper to taste

Season the onions with salt and let them sit for half an hour. Combine the water, olive oil and vinegar and season with pepper. Pour the dressing over the onion and allow to sit for ten minutes. Place the tomatoes in a serving dish and cover with the onions and the dressing. Season with salt and pepper again if desired.

*

*

BEET SALAD WITH TOMATOES
(The Ukraine)

1 lb. pickled beets, sliced
3 tomatoes, sliced
1 clove of garlic, minced

4 tbsp. olive oil
1 onion, finely chopped
2 tbsp. vinegar
salt and pepper to taste

Place the onion, tomatoes and beets in a dish. Combine the remaining ingredients to form a dressing. Pour the dressing over the salad and let it sit for twenty minutes before serving.

*

CARROT AND CABBAGE SALAD
(Russia)

2 c. grated carrot
1 tbsp. wine vinegar
1 c. sour cream

1 c. cabbage, shredded
1 tsp. sugar
salt and pepper to taste

Salt the cabbage and let sit for half an hour. Combine the cabbage and the carrot in a serving bowl. Mix together the sour cream, sugar and vinegar. Season with salt and pepper. Add this dressing to the salad and mix well.

*

*

SPINACH SALAD
(The Ukraine)

1 lb. spinach
1 clove of garlic, diced
2 tbsp. vinegar
4 tbsp. olive oil

2 hard-cooked eggs,
   chopped
¼ tsp. paprika
salt and pepper to taste

Wash and dry the spinach. Tear the leaves and place in a bowl with the hard-cooked eggs. Combine the remaining ingredients to make a dressing. Pour the dressing over the salad and serve.

*

POTATO SALAD
(Poland)

5 potatoes
½ c. celery, finely chopped
2 tsp. capers, crushed
2 hard-cooked eggs
¼ c. green pepper, diced
¼ c. pickles, chopped
2 tbsp. vinegar

1 onion, finely chopped
½ c. beets, diced
1 tbsp. parsley, chopped
½ c. Polish sausage,
   cooked and cubed
1½ c. sour cream
salt and pepper to taste

Boil and cube the potatoes. Chop the eggs. Combine the potatoes, celery, eggs, green pepper, pickle, onion, beets and Polish sausage in a bowl. Mix together the sour cream, vinegar, parsley and capers. Season with salt and pepper. Add the sour cream dressing to the salad and mix well. Chill and serve.

*

SHOPSKA SALAD
(Bulgaria)

2 green peppers, sliced	½ c. feta cheese
2 red peppers, sliced	5 tbsp. olive oil
4 tomatoes, thinly sliced	2 tbsp. lemon juice
2 onions, sliced	2 tbsp. chopped parsley
1 cucumber, sliced	1 tbsp. dill, finely chopped
	salt and pepper to taste

Place the vegetables in layers on a plate or in a bowl. Combine the oil, lemon juice, dill, parsley, salt and pepper. Mix well. Pour this dressing over the salad and top with the cheese. Serves 6.

*

GREEN BEAN AND ARTICHOKE SALAD
(Croatia)

4 artichokes	1 lb. green beans
4 tbsp. butter	½ tsp. garlic powder
	salt to taste

Wash the artichokes and remove the stems and leaf ends. Place in a pot with enough water to cover. Add one tablespoon of salt and cook for 35-45 minutes until tender. Drain. Cube the artichokes and cook for another five minutes in a little water. Wash and clean the green beans and cook for twenty minutes to half an hour until tender. Drain the green beans and place them in a large serving bowl. Melt the butter over low heat. Pour the butter over the green beans. Garnish by arranging the artichokes around the green beans. Season with garlic powder and more salt, if desired. Serves 4-5.

*

YOGHURT DRESSING
(Bulgaria)

½ c. yoghurt
1 tbsp. lemon juice

2 tbsp. olive oil
salt and pepper to taste

Combine the yoghurt, olive oil and lemon juice. Season with salt and pepper. Mix well and pour over the salad.

*

WHITE WINE DRESSING
(Croatia)

3 tbsp. olive oil
3 tbsp. white wine

1 tsp. lemon juice
½ tsp. paprika
salt and pepper to taste

Add the seasonings to the oil. Add the wine and mix well. Add the lemon juice drop by drop, stirring constantly. Use with any green salad.

＊

RUSSIAN DRESSING
(Russia)

2 egg yolks
¼ tsp. paprika
1 c. salad oil
1 tbsp. Worcestershire
   sauce

¼ tsp. mustard
4 tbsp. lemon juice
1 tbsp. chili sauce
1 tbsp. chopped pimentos
salt and pepper to taste

Mix together the egg yolks, lemon juice, paprika and mustard. Slowly pour in the salad oil, beating vigorously after each addition, to make a rich mayonnaise. Add the chopped pimentos, Worcestershire sauce and chili sauce. Mix well and season with salt and pepper.

＊

GARLIC DRESSING
(The Ukraine)

1 tsp. minced garlic
2 tbsp. vinegar

4 tbsp. olive oil
1 tbsp. chopped parsley
salt and pepper to taste

Combine the oil and vinegar. Add the garlic and parsley. Season with salt and pepper. Let the dressing sit for an hour or two. Shake well and pour over salad.

*

HOT BACON DRESSING
(Czechoslovakia)

½ c. bacon, diced   2 tbsp. vinegar
¼ c. water   ½ tsp. sugar
                             salt and pepper to taste

Combine the water, sugar and vinegar. Season with salt and pepper. Pour the mixture over green salad. Fry the bacon in a skillet until crisp. Pour the hot bacon and rendered fat over the salad and serve.

*

MAYONNAISE AND DILL DRESSING
(Poland)

2 egg yolks   1 c. salad oil
¼ tsp. mustard   2 tbsp. lemon juice
¼ tsp. paprika   2 tbsp. dill, finely chopped
1 tbsp. chopped parsley   salt and pepper to taste

Mix together the egg yolks, lemon juice, paprika and mustard. Slowly add the oil, a little at a time, beating vigorously after each addition to make a rich mayonnaise. Stir in the dill and parsley. Season with salt and pepper and blend well.

*

SOUR CREAM DRESSING
(Croatia)

1 c. sour cream	1 tbsp. lemon juice
1 egg yolk	1 tbsp. ground parsley
1 tbsp. mustard	salt and pepper to taste

Combine the sour cream, egg yolk and mustard. Add the lemon juice and season with salt and pepper. Whip until very smooth and creamy. If necessary, dilute with a few drops of milk. Stir in the ground parsley just before serving. Do not allow this dressing to sit on the salad. Sour Cream Dressing is especially good on potato salad.

VEGETABLES

VEGETABLES

*

SAUTEED KOHLRABI
(Czechoslovakia)

2 lbs. kohlrabi	1 onion, chopped
4 tbsp. butter	¼ tsp. caraway seeds
1 tbsp. flour	1 tsp. sugar
2 tsp. vinegar	salt to taste

Melt the butter in a saucepan and saute the onion. Peel the kohlrabi and cut into strips. Add the kohlrabi and caraway seeds to the onion. Season with salt. Saute the kohlrabi for fifteen minutes. Combine the vinegar, sugar and flour and add to 1 cup of water. Add the water to the kohlrabi and bring to a boil. Serves 6.

*

BAKED ZUCCHINI
(Croatia)

1 lb. zucchini	½ c. grated cheese
1 c. water	½ c. sour cream
½ tbsp. vinegar	½ c. butter
	2 egg yolks, well beaten

Wash the zucchini. Snip off the ends and grate coarsely. Cook the zucchini in water to which the vinegar has been added. When tender, remove from heat and drain the excess water. Grease a deep baking dish and place the zucchini in it. Combine the egg yolks, butter, sour cream and cheese. Cook until a thick sauce forms. Pour this sauce over the zucchini. Place the zucchini in a hot oven (450°) and bake for 8-12 minutes until the top begins to brown. Serves 4.

*

PEAS WITH BARLEY
(The Ukraine)

2 c. peas   1 onion, finely chopped
2 c. barley   4 tbsp. oil
½ c. bacon, diced   salt to taste

Cook the peas and barley separately until tender in salted water, then combine. Fry the diced bacon and saute the onion in it. Add the barley, peas and oil. Season with salt. Cook the barley and peas for five to ten minutes. Serves 6.

*

*

SAUTEED KALE
(Czechoslovakia)

2 lbs. kale

¼ c. bacon, diced

1 onion, finely chopped

4 tbsp. flour

salt and pepper to taste

Place the bacon in a skillet and fry with the onion. Add the kale and saute for fifteen minutes. Combine the flour with one cup of water and add to the kale. Season with salt and pepper. Cook for another five minutes until the sauce thickens. Serves 6.

*

ZUCCHINI AND EGGPLANT
(Bulgaria)

3 eggplants

4 zucchinis, sliced

¼ c. flour

¾ c. oil

1 tbsp. garlic, chopped

1 c. walnuts, chopped

½ c. yoghurt

salt and pepper to taste

Slice the eggplants and allow them to drain for half an hour. Salt both the zucchinis and the eggplants. Dip in flour and fry the slices in oil until well done. Combine the garlic, walnuts and yoghurt. Season with salt and pepper. Pour this sauce over the vegetables and serve. Serves 5-6.

*

BAKED EGGPLANT
(Russia)

1 eggplant, peeled
1 tbsp. flour
2 tbsp. butter

2 c. milk
2 tbsp. Parmesan cheese,
   grated
salt and pepper to taste

Thickly slice the eggplant and boil in salted water for five minutes. Drain the slices and place in a buttered casserole dish. Heat the butter in a saucepan and add the flour to make a golden roux. Season with salt and pepper. Slowly pour in the milk, stirring constantly. Pour this sauce over the eggplant and sprinkle with grated cheese. Bake in a moderate oven at 350° for half an hour. Serves 4.

*

COOKED BEANS
(Bulgaria)

1 c. navy beans
1 onion, finely chopped
1 clove garlic, diced
1 tsp. vinegar

3 tbsp. olive oil
1 tbsp. flour
3 tbsp. tomato paste
1 tsp. parsley, minced
salt and pepper to taste

Cook the beans in salted water for two hour or until tender. Drain the beans and save the liquid. Heat the olive oil and fry the onion and garlic in it for five to ten minutes. Add the tomato paste, parsley, vinegar, flour and a little of the liquid that the beans cooked in. Season with salt and pepper. Add the beans and allow to cook for five minutes longer. Serves 4.

*

MUSHROOMS WITH BACON
(Russia)

1 lb. mushrooms, sliced   ¼ lb. bacon, diced
2 tbsp. sour cream   salt and pepper to taste

Fry the bacon in its own fat until crisp. Add the mushrooms and season with salt and pepper. Cook until tender. Allow the mushrooms to cool and then stir in the sour cream. Serves 4.

*

POTATO PANCAKES
(The Ukraine)

2 c. potatoes, grated   2 eggs, well beaten
1 tbsp. flour   1 onion, finely chopped

4 tbsp. butter   salt and pepper to taste
                                dash of paprika

Drain the potatoes well. Add the eggs, flour and onions. Season with salt and pepper and mix well. Heat half the butter in a skillet over medium heat; increase the heat until butter foams. Pour in the potato batter one spoonful at a time and fry until brown. Flip each pancake over and allow the other side to turn a golden brown. Sprinkle each pancake with paprika before serving. Serves 4.

*

CAULIFLOWER À LA POLONAISE
(Poland)

1 head of cauliflower   4 tbsp. butter
¼ c. breadcrumbs   salted water

Cook the cauliflower in salted water and break into flowerets. Heat the butter in a skillet and fry the bread-crumbs in it. Allow the breadcrumbs to brown and then pour the butter and breadcrumbs over the cauliflower. Serves 4

*

*

PICKLED MUSHROOMS
(Czechoslovakia)

4 lbs. mushrooms   8 tbsp. vinegar
2 bay leaves   8 peppercorns
2 c. water   1 tsp. sugar
1 tsp. mustard seeds   salt to taste

Wash and quarter the mushrooms and cook them in salted water for five minutes. Combine the vinegar, water, peppercorns and bay leaves. Simmer for five minutes. Place the mushrooms in canning jars and sprinkle with mustard seeds. Pour equal amounts of the vinegar and spices into each jar. Close the jars and store for at a week.

*

POLISH CABBAGE
(Poland)

1 head of cabbage,   3 tbsp. vinegar
   shredded   1 onion, chopped
2 tbsp. flour   2 tbsp. butter
                         salt and pepper to taste

Salt the cabbage and allow to sit for an hour. Squeeze out any excess water and cook in cold water and vinegar until soft. Season with salt and pepper. Heat the butter in

---

saucepan and brown the onion in it. Add the flour and a little water to make a sauce. Season with salt. Pour the sauce over the cabbage and serve. Serves 4.

*

COOKED LENTILS
(Bulgaria)

1 lb. yellow lentils   3 tbsp. butter
1 ham bone   1 onion, finely chopped
                              salt and pepper to taste

Place the lentils and ham bone in salted water and cook for two or three hours or until tender. They should break easily when done. Melt the butter in a skillet and saute the onion until tender. Add the lentils and season with salt and pepper. Allow to cook for another fifteen minutes. Serves 5-6.

*

*

BEETS WITH SOUR CREAM
(Poland)

5 large beets
2 tbsp. butter
½ tsp. caraway seeds
½ c. sour cream

1 tbsp. flour
1 tbsp. vinegar
1 tbsp. sugar
salt to taste

Boil the beets in salted water until tender. Drain the beets, peel and grate. Heat the butter in a saucepan and add in the caraway seeds and vinegar. Season with salt and sugar. Add the beets and flour and stir well. Allow to cook for five minutes. Stir in the sour cream and serve. Serves 6.

*

PEAS IN A NEST
(Croatia)

6-8 cooked potatoes
2 c. cooked peas
¼ c. milk
2 tbsp. butter or oil

¼ c. smoked bacon
dash of nutmeg
¼ c. sour cream
salt to taste

Mash the potatoes with the butter and nutmeg. Season with salt. Add the milk and mash well. Finely dice the bacon. Line the bottom of individual ovenproof glass serving dishes with it. Fill the dishes with mashed potatoes. Leave a well in the center for the cooked peas. Add the cooked peas to the centers and dab each with a little butter. Bake at 400° for eight to ten minutes. Garnish each nest with a teaspoon of sour cream and serve immediately. Serves 6.

*

POTATOES IN SOUR CREAM
(Russia)

3 lbs. potatoes, peeled   ¾ c. sour cream
3 tsp. parsley

Boil the potatoes in salted water until tender. Quarter the potatoes and place in a saucepan. Add the sour cream and parsley. Mix well and allow to cook over low heat for five minutes. Serves 6.

*

SPINACH WITH SOUR CREAM
(Poland)

2 lb. cooked spinach,   1 onion, finely chopped
  finely chopped   4 tbsp. Parmesan cheese
1 c. sour cream   salt and pepper to taste
2 tbsp. butter

Heat the butter in a saucepan. Add the onion and saute for five minutes. Add the spinach. Allow it to simmer for another two to three minutes. Season with salt and pepper. Stir in the sour cream and grated cheese and allow to simmer for another five minutes. Serves 6.

*

KASHA, BUCKWHEAT GROATS
(Russia)

1 c. buckwheat groats   3 c. water
½ tsp. salt   4 tbsp. butter
1 onion, finely chopped

Heat the water and bring to a boil; add the buckwheat groats and salt. Bring to a boil and then simmer over low heat for 45 minutes. When the kasha is soft, but not mushy, it is ready. Heat the butter and saute the onion in it. Add the kasha and mix well. Serve immediately. Serves 4.

*

SUMMER SQUASH
(Bulgaria)

1½ lbs. summer squash   1 onion, finely chopped
2 tbsp. butter   2 tbsp. vinegar
1 tsp. sugar   ½ c. water

1 tsp. dill, chopped   ½ c. sour cream
1 clove garlic, diced   salt to taste

Peel and cube the squash. Heat the butter in a saucepan and saute the onion and garlic in it until tender. Add the squash and fry for five minutes. Season with salt. Stir in the water, vinegar, sugar and dill. Allow to cook for fifteen to twenty minutes or until the squash is tender. Stir in the sour cream and simmer for an additional minute. Serve immediately. Serves 4.

*

STEWED PUMPKIN
(Slovenia)

2 lbs. pumpkin   ½ tsp. chopped parsley
3 tbsp. butter   1 tsp. sugar
                             salt to taste

Cook the pumpkin in salted water until tender. Slice thinly. Heat the butter in a skillet and add the pumpkin, parsley and sugar. Season with salt. Allow the pumpkin to simmer for about ten minutes in the butter. Serves 6.

*

*

CREAMED GREEN PEAS
(Czechoslovakia)

1 lb. fresh green peas	4 tbsp. butter
2 tbsp. flour	1 c. cream
1 tsp. parsley, chopped	salt to taste

Place the peas in salted water and cook for about ten minutes. Heat the butter and add the cooked peas. Season with salt and saute in the butter for five minutes. Combine the cream, flour and parsley. Add this mixture to the peas, stirring well. Allow to cook slowly for another five minutes. Serves 4.

*

MUSHROOMS AND SPINACH
(Croatia)

2 lbs. sliced mushrooms	¾ lb. chopped spinach
1 tbsp. minced parsley	1 onion, finely chopped
2 slices bread	1 tbsp. olive oil
¾ c. sour cream	salt and pepper to taste

Combine the mushrooms with the bread slices which have been soaked in milk. Add the parsley. Cook this mixture over medium heat in a little salted water for about five minutes. Add the spinach and continue to cook over low heat until the liquid evaporates. Saute the onion in the oil until it begins to brown. Add the mushroom and spinach mixture. Cook for about five minutes. Stir in the sour cream. Season with salt and pepper. Serves 6.

*

CABBAGE WITH SOUR CREAM
(Russia)

1 head of cabbage, shredded	2 tbsp. butter
1 tbsp. flour	1 c. sour cream
	salt and pepper to taste

Cook the cabbage in salted water until tender. Melt the butter in a saucepan and add the flour and sour cream. Season with salt and pepper. Add the cabbage and cook slowly for ten to fifteen minutes. Serves 6.

*

SAUERKRAUT WITH CARAWAY SEEDS
(Czechoslovakia)

1 lb. sauerkraut	½ tsp. dry mustard
¼ c. red wine	1 tbsp. sugar
2 tsp. caraway seeds	¼ lb. Polish sausage, sliced

Combine the sauerkraut, sausage, wine, caraway seeds, dry mustard and sugar in a saucepan. Cover the saucepan and allow to simmer for two hours. Shake gently from time to time to keep from sticking. Serves 4.

*

BREADED MUSHROOMS
(Croatia)

2 lbs. mushrooms	¾ c. breadcrumbs
3 tbsp. flour	1 c. butter
2 eggs, well beaten	1 c. oil
fresh parsley	salt and pepper to taste

Wash the mushrooms well. Remove the stalks. Season the heads with salt and pepper. Roll each mushroom head in flour, dip in egg and roll in the breadcrumbs. Be sure that the coating is thick and smooth. Heat the butter and oil in a large skillet and fry the mushrooms until golden. Fry each mushroom immediately as it is coated with the flour, egg and breadcrumbs so that the coating does not fall off. Serve the fried mushrooms on a bed of steamed rice and garnish with sprigs of fresh parsley. Breaded mushrooms may be served with a small bowl of sour cream. Serves 6.

*

*

CABBAGE WITH APPLES
(Poland)

1 head red cabbage   1 apple
1 onion, finely chopped   2 tbsp. vinegar
1 tbsp. sugar   1 tbsp. flour
1 c. water   salt and pepper to taste

Shred and salt the cabbage and allow it to sit for an hour. Peel and slice the apple. Heat the water in a saucepan and add the cabbage, apple, sugar, onion and vinegar. Season with pepper and cook for half an hour or until the cabbage is tender. Add water as needed. Add the flour when the cabbage is done and cook for five to ten minutes longer. Serves 5-6.

*

CHEESE POTATOES
(Croatia)

2 lbs. potatoes   ¾ c. sour cream
¾ lb. cottage cheese   ¼ lb. sliced smoked bacon
                            salt and pepper to taste

Peel the potatoes and cook in salted, boiling water until tender. Fry half the bacon in its own fat. Cover the bottom of a baking dish with the fried bacon. Place half the cooked potatoes over the bacon. Season with salt and pepper. Combine the cheese and sour cream. Place this mixture over the potatoes. Add the remaining potatoes. Season with salt and pepper. Bake in a hot over (450°) for an hour and a half to two hours. Cover the top of the potatoes with the remaining slices of smoked bacon. Return to the oven and continue to bake until the bacon is very well done. Serve immediately. Serves 6.

DESSERTS

DESSERTS

*

CHARLOTTKA
(Russia)

15 ladyfingers
½ c. sugar
2 packages unflavored
  gelatin
½ c. cream, chilled

4 egg yolks
1 c. warm milk
3 tbsp. water
½ c. sour cream, chilled
1 tsp. vanilla

Cut the ladyfingers in half lengthwise. Dissolve the gelatin in the water. Cut enough ladyfingers into full length triangles and use to line the bottom of a charlotte mold. Place the triangles in the bottom of the mold pointing toward the center. Use the remaining ladyfinger halves to stand next to each other along the wall of the charlotte mold. Beat the egg yolks well and add in the sugar beating constantly. Add the vanilla to the milk. Add the milk to the eggs, beating constantly. Cook the mixture over low heat or in a double boiler until the mixture thickens into a smooth custard. Do not allow the custard to boil. Remove from heat and add in the dissolved gelatin. Combine the sour cream and the sweet cream and beat until thick. Place the pan of custard in the refrigerator to chill. When it has cooled, but has not yet set, fold in the beaten cream. Gently stir until well mixed. Pour the custard and cream mixture into the charlotte mold and smooth the top. Trim off the ladyfingers if the ends stand above the level of the custard. Place the mold in the refrigerator to chill. Chill the Charlottka for five to six hours.

Remove from the refrigerator and place a flat inverted cake stand on top. Hold firmly together both the cake and the mold and flip it over. Remove the mold. Garnish the Charlottka with whipped cream and serve. For variation the Charlottka can also be flavored with chocolate or by adding mashed fruit such as pineapples or strawberries to the custard.

*

BASIC PALAČINKE
(Croatia)

3 eggs	1 c. milk
1¼ c. flour	½ tsp. salt
	¼ c. butter

Make a smooth pancake batter by mixing the eggs, flour, milk and salt. Allow the batter to sit for approximately half an hour. Spoon the batter onto a pancake skillet, well greased with a small pat of butter. Tip and roll the skillet until a thin layer of batter covers the bottom. When the batter bubbles turn the palačinka over and brown the other side. Remove to a warm plate. Add butter to the skillet and continue making palačinke until all the batter is used up. Place the palačinke in a warm oven until the filling is ready if you are using cheese filling or allow the pancakes to cool slightly if cream filling is used.

CREAM FILLING:

¼ c. ground walnuts   1 c. whipped cream
                             ½ tsp. vanilla

Chocolate Sauce:

1 c. sugar   1 square chocolate, grated
½ c. water   1 tbsp. butter

Allow the pancakes to cool for about five minutes after they are fried. Whip the cream. Mix the cream, walnuts and vanilla. Spread each pancake with this mixture and roll it up. Arrange the filled pancakes on a serving platter. Mix together the sugar, water and grated chocolate to make a sauce. Boil for five minutes in the top of a double boiler. Allow the sauce to cool until it is warm, then stir in the butter. Mix well. Pour this chocolate sauce over the palačinke. Sprinkle with confectioner's sugar and coarsely ground walnuts.

CHEESE FILLING:

1 lb. cottage cheese   1 egg
3 tbsp. sugar   ½ tsp. vanilla

Beat the egg. Add the remaining ingredients and mix well. Spread each palačinka with the cheese filling and roll it up into a cylinder. Place the filled palacinke in a shallow baking dish as they are made. Place the dish in the oven at 425° for about ten to fifteen minutes. Serve hot.

*

*

ALMOND MOUSSE
(Czechoslovakia)

1½ c. ground almonds   ½ c. sugar
½ c. milk   1½ c. whipped cream
1 tbsp. cocoa   2 tbsp. gelatin
¼ c. water

Heat the milk. Add the cocoa and the almonds, cooking for ten to fifteen minutes. Dissolve the gelatin in a tablespoon of water and add it to the milk. Chill the milk and then stir in the sugar and the whipped cream. Wet a dessert mold with water and pour in the mixture. Place the mousse in the freezer of the refrigerator for three hours. When ready to serve, dip the mold in warm water to loosen the mousse. Turn the mousse over onto a serving dish. Serves 5-6.

*

FILLED BAKED APPLES
(The Ukraine)

6 apples   6 tbsp. sugar
2 tbsp. almonds, chopped   1 tsp. cinnamon
½ c. raisins   2 tbsp. rum
   whipped cream

Combine the almonds, raisins, cinnamon, sugar and rum.
Core the apples and remove a little pulp to make a cavity.
Fill the apples with the almond and raisins mixture. Place
the apples in a baking dish. Cover the bottom of the dish
with water. Bake the apples in a moderate oven at 350° until
tender. When the apples are done, remove and refrigerate.
When cold, garnish each apple with whipped cream and a
candied cherry. Serves 6.

*

CRANBERRY KISSEL
(Russia)

4 c. cranberries	2 tbsp. cornstarch
2 c. sugar	2 c. water
½ tsp. cinnamon	whipped cream

Wash the cranberries and boil in the water. Allow the
cranberries to cook for ten minutes. Pass them through a
sieve to make a puree. Place the cranberry puree in a
saucepan and add the sugar, cinnamon and cornstarch
mixed with a little water. Bring the mixture to a boil and
cook for five minutes, stirring constantly. Pour the kissel into
individual dessert dishes and place in the refrigerator to
cool. When ready, garnish with whipped cream. Serves 8.

*

*

PASKHA
(Russia)

7 c. cottage cheese	2 c. butter
½ c. raisins	2 tsp. vanilla
2 c. sugar	3 eggs, well beaten

Mash the cottage cheese and stir in the butter. Mix well so that the butter is well blended and that the cheese becomes smooth. Add the eggs, sugar and vanilla. Beat the mixture vigorously until it is very smooth. Line a colander with two layers of cheesecloth. Lay a layer of raisins on the cheesecloth. Pour in the cottage cheese mixture and fold over the cheesecloth to cover the cheese. Place a flat tin or pan on the cheese and a dish under the colander. Place this in the refrigerator for one or two days. This allows excess water to drain from the paskha. Place a heavy weight on the tin or dish on top of the cheese. Remove the paskha from the refrigerator and flip over onto a serving dish. Serves 6.

*

CINNAMON PEARS
(Poland)

6 pears	½ c. sugar
1 c. water	½ tsp. cinnamon
whipped cream	1 tbsp. butter

Peel the pears and slice in half. Remove the cores. Melt the butter in a saucepan and brown the sugar, stirring constantly. Add the water, cinnamon and pears. Cook until the pears are tender. Place the pears in individual dessert dishes and cover with sauce. Refrigerate for about two to three hours. When ready to serve, garnish with whipped cream.

*

FRUIT SALAD WITH WINE
(Bulgaria)

1 c. cherries	3 peaches
1 c. seedless grapes	2 apples
2 pears	2 c. dessert wine,
½ c. walnuts, chopped	(Marsala or Muscatel)
½ cantaloupe, cubed	¼ c. brandy
	1 tbsp. sugar

Halve the cherries and remove the pits. Peel and cube the apples, pears, peaches and cantaloupe. Halve the grapes. Combine the fruit in a serving bowl. Add the walnuts. Mix together the sugar, brandy and wine. Pour this over the fruit and refrigerate for several hours. If desired, place the fruit salad into individual serving dishes. Serves 6.

*

---

*

STEWED PEACHES
(Slovenia)

6 peaches   3 tbsp. maraschino liqueur
3 tbsp. sugar   ½ c. water

*Peel and halve the peaches. Remove the pit. Add the sugar
and maraschino liqueur to the water and pour into a
saucepan. Place the peaches into this sauce and simmer
over low heat until the fruit is tender. Serve warm or chill and
garnish with whipped cream. Serves 6.*

*

STRAWBERRY FROTH
(Croatia)

4 c. strawberries   1 c. sugar
                              1 c. whipping cream

*Sieve the berries, saving a few for garnish. Add the sugar
and mix well. Whip the cream. Combine the fruit and 3/4 of
the whipped cream. Place in parfait glasses. Refrigerate for
at least three hours. Garnish with the remaining whipped
cream and the whole berries before serving. Serves 6.*

*

*

STRAWBERRIES ROMANOFF
(Russia)

1 lb. strawberries	1½ tbsp. curacao
1 c. sugar	2 tbsp. orange juice
½ tbsp. grated orange peel	1 c. cream

Rinse and hull the strawberries and then dry well. Combine the sugar, curacao, orange juice and orange peel. Pour this mixture over the strawberries and refrigerate for several hours. Beat the cream well and place alternate layers of strawberries and whipped cream in serving glasses. Top off with whipped cream. Serves 4.

*

DEEP-FRIED CHESTNUT BALLS
(Bulgaria)

2 lb. chestnuts	1 c. powdered sugar
¾ c. milk	oil for deep frying
	confectioner's sugar

Shell the chestnuts and boil in water until soft. Remove the chestnuts and mash well. Slowly add the milk and sugar to the chestnuts. Work into a thick dough, adjusting the milk as necessary. Break off dough and roll into one inch balls. Heat the oil and deep fry the chestnuts balls. Remove from the oil and drain. Dredge in powdered sugar.

---

*

APRICOT AND PEACH SAUCE
(Slovenia)

½ lb. apricots   1 c. water
½ lb. peaches   ½ c. sugar
                          whipped cream

*Peel and halve both the apricots and the peaches. Remove
the pits and finely chop. Mash the fruit well. Heat the water
and add the sugar and fruit. Cook until the sauce thickens.
Chill the fruit sauce and serve with whipped cream.
Serves 4.*

*

STEAMED FIGS
(Bulgaria)

20 figs   2 tbsp. water
4 tbsp. powdered sugar   whipped cream

*Wash the figs and remove the stems. Cover with water and
soak for 2-3 hours. Place two tablespoons of water in a
double boiler and add the figs, cooking until tender. Place
the figs in individual dessert dishes and sprinkle with sugar.
Garnish with whipped cream. Serves 4-6.*

*

*

CHERRY DUMPLINGS
(The Ukraine)

4 c. flour, sifted	4 c. pitted cherries
1 c. water	2 tsp. salt
4 eggs, slightly beaten	½ c. sugar
2 tbsp. butter	

Sift the salt and flour together. Place the flour on a board and make a well in the center. Place the eggs in the center, along with half the water. Begin to work the flour into a firm dough. Add more water, as required, and continue to knead until the dough is smooth and elastic. Cover the dough with a cloth and allow it to sit for an hour. Heat the butter in a saucepan and add the cherries and sugar. Saute the cherries for five to ten minutes, being careful not let the sugar burn. Flour a board and roll out the dough. Cut into 3 inch squares. Place a teaspoonful of the cherries on the dough. Wet the edges of the dough, fold over and press to close well. Cook the dumplings in boiling water for 20 minutes. Drain and serve sprinkled with powdered sugar. Serves 6-8.

*

RAISIN AND RICE PUDDING
(Bulgaria)

½ c. raisins	½ c. sugar
¼ c. cooked rice	¼ tsp. cinnamon

5 c. milk   4 tbsp. cornstarch
                             whipped cream

Scald the milk and remove from heat. Add the raisins and allow them to soak in the warm milk for twenty minutes. Pour the milk into a large saucepan or the top of a double boiler; stir in the cornstarch and mix well. Add the rice, sugar and cinnamon. Bring the pudding to a boil over low heat and cook until thick. Stir the pudding constantly and do not allow to stick. Pour the pudding into individual serving dishes and chill in the refrigerator until the pudding is firm. Garnish with whipped cream. Serves 6.

*

KUTIA
(Poland)

2 c. whole wheat grain   5 c. water
2 c. poppy seeds   ½ c. ground almonds
5 tbsp. cream   2 tbsp. honey

Wash the wheat grain well. Heat the water to a boil and add the grain. Cook for five minutes and drain. Heat fresh water, add the grain and boil for two hours or until tender. Add water if necessary, do not allow to thicken. Drain the grain. Heat enough water to cook the poppy seeds, and cook for two to three minutes; remove from heat and allow to sit in the water for one hour. Drain the seeds and mash well. Add the cream to the poppy seeds. Stir this mixture into the wheat grain when cooled. Add the honey and almonds. Mix well and refrigerate. This is served as traditional Christmas Eve dessert. Serves 5-6.

*

MILK KISSEL
(The Ukraine)

4 c. milk
½ c. sugar

2 tbsp. cornstarch
½ tsp. vanilla

Heat the milk and bring to a boil. Dissolve the cornstarch in a little cold milk. Add the cornstarch, sugar and vanilla to the milk. Bring the milk to a boil and cook for five minutes over low heat. Pour the milk kissel into individual dessert dishes and chill. Serves 6.

*

FILBERT PARFAIT
(Croatia)

3 c. whipped cream
¼ c. sugar

1½ c. ground filberts
3 packets gelatin
¼ c. pistachios, chopped

Melt the gelatin in a little warm water. Brown the filberts in an ungreased pan, stirring constantly. Beat the gelatin, sugar and filberts into the whipped cream. Pour this mixture into a mold or individual parfait glasses. Refrigerate for at least two hours. Garnish with the remaining whipped cream and chopped pistachios. Serves 6.

*

*

CHOCOLATE PUDDING
(Czechoslovakia)

2 squares semi-sweet chocolate, melted	1 c. milk
	½ c. sugar
8 egg whites, well beaten	½ tsp. vanilla
8 egg yolks	¼ c. breadcrumbs

Heat the milk and stir in the chocolate. Add the breadcrumbs, sugar and vanilla. Beat the mixture until it thickens. Allow the milk and chocolate mixture to cool. Add the egg yolks, one at a time, and beat vigorously with each addition. Slowly fold in the stiffly beaten egg whites. Butter a bainmarie and steam the pudding for one hour. Serves 6.

*

COFFEE CREAM
(Poland)

1 c. coffee	¼ c. water
2 c. cream	1 c. sugar
2 packages gelatin	sweet chocolate, grated

Dissolve the gelatin in the water. Beat the cream until it thickens. Add the sugar, dissolved gelatin and coffee. Mix well. Pour into a mold or into individual dessert dishes. Refrigerate the cream for several hours or overnight. Serve sprinkled with grated chocolate. The stronger the coffee, the stronger the flavor of the cream. Serves 6.

PASTRIES

PASTRIES

*

SAVIJAĆA
(Croatia)

4 c. flour	1 tbsp. vinegar
1 tsp. salt	2 tbsp. oil
1 egg	1¼ c. warm water, approx.

Sift the flour and salt into a large mixing bowl twice. Make a
well in the center. Drop in the egg, vinegar and oil and mix
the ingredients well. Add one cup warm water. Work all the
ingredients into a firm dough. Add more water as required
to make a smooth and elastic dough. Continue to knead the
dough until it is soft and begins to blister. Experience will
help you decide when the dough is soft enough. The dough
must be very soft, but smooth enough not to stick to the
hands. Divide the dough into two balls. Grease a deep bowl
with butter or margarine. Place the balls of dough in the
bowl. Turn them around so that they will be greased on all
sides. Cover the bowl with a damp kitchen towel and allow it
to rest in a warm place for approximately an hour. Spread a
large table with a tablecloth. Dust generousy with flour. Roll
one of the balls of dough very thin with a rolling pin. Brush
with a little oil. Begin stretching the dough by pulling from
the center out with floured fists. Pull the dough in all
directions. When the dough covers more than half the table
and the center is very thin, begin pulling the edges with the
fingertips. Walk around the table, always pulling from the
center. Be sure to pull the dough evenly from all sides. When

the dough is fully stretched, it should cover the whole table and should be thin enough to read newsprint through it. Allow the dough to drape over the edges of the table. Trim the edges with kitchen shears or tear the thick edges away gently. Allow the dough to dry for ten to fifteen minutes. Brush the dough generously with the melted butter, then spread half the filling over two thirds of the dough. Gently lift the tablecloth at that end of the table where the dough has been spread with filling. Pull the tablecloth so that the dough will roll as the tablecloth is pulled upward toward you. The rolled savijaca will look like a large snake. Place on a cookie sheet and brush the top of the savijaca with a little melted butter. Stretch, fill and roll the other ball of dough. Brush with melted butter. Bake in a hot oven at 425° for ten minutes. Reduce the heat and bake at 350° until the savijaca is golden brown. Remove from the oven and allow to cool slightly before cutting into serving sized portions. Dust the savijaca with confectioner's sugar before serving. Serve either hot or cold.

Cherry Filling:

2 c. pitted cherries	¼ c. fine breadcrumbs
¼ c. water	¼ c. butter
½ c. sugar	¼ c. sliced almonds

Cook the cherries for fifteen minutes in the sugar and water. Drain. Spread the stretched savijaca dough with the melted butter. Sprinkle with breadcrumbs and almond slices. Spread the cherries over two thirds of the dough, dropping a spoonful at a time. If desired, canned cherry pie filling may be substituted for fresh cherries. Roll and bake the savijaca as directed above.

Cheese Filling:

2 lbs. cottage cheese	¼ c. sugar
3 tbsp. sweet cream	2 eggs
¼ c. melted butter	¼ c. raisins (optionally)

Combine the cheese with the cream. Beat the eggs and add to the cheese mixture. Beat in the sugar and raisins, if used. Brush the savijaca dough with the melted butter. Spread two thirds of the dough with the cheese filling. Roll and bake as directed above.

Apple Filling:

3 c. tart apples, thinly sliced	½ c. sugar
¼ c. melted butter	¼ c. fine breadcrumbs
¼ c. sliced almonds	1 tsp. cinnamon

Brush the stretched savijaca dough with melted butter. Sprinkle with breadcrumbs and sliced almonds. Spread the apple slices over two-thirds of the dough. Sprinkle with sugar and cinnamon. Roll and bake the savijaca as directed above.

*

ROLLED OAT COOKIES
(Czechoslovakia)

2 c. sifted flour	1½ c. brown sugar
1½ c. rolled oats	½ tsp. salt

½ tsp. baking soda
⅔ c. milk
2 tsp. baking powder
½ c. raisins
½ c. dates, chopped

2 eggs, well beaten
1 tsp. vanilla
1 c. shortening
1 c. filberts, chopped

Sift together the flour, salt, baking powder and baking soda. Cream together the brown sugar, shortening and eggs. Slowly add the dry ingredients and the milk, alternating with each addition. Add the dates, vanilla, raisins, nuts and rolled oats. Mix the batter well. Place the batter in small mounds onto a greased cookie sheet and bake at 350° until golden brown.

*

KHVOROST
(Russia)

3 c. flour, sifted
3 eggs, lightly beaten
½ c. water
2 tbsp. vodka

½ c. sugar
½ tsp. salt
confectioner's sugar
fat for deep frying

Place the flour in a bowl. Add the eggs, water, vodka, salt and sugar. Blend well and work into a smooth firm dough. Roll the dough out flat onto a floured board. Cut into one-inch strips about four inches long. Cut a slit in the middle of each strip and pull one end of the strip throuh the slit to make a loop. Heat the oil and drop the strips into the hot oil to deep fry. When the strips are a golden brown remove and drain. Sprinkle with confectioner's sugar and serve hot or cold.

*

POPPY-SEED CAKE
(The Ukraine)

1 c. cornstarch	1 c. poppy seeds
15 egg yolks, well beaten	1 c. sugar
2 c. sweet cream	½ c. almonds, chopped
9 egg whites, stiffly beaten	1 c. milk
2 tbsp. butter	3 tbsp. breadcrumbs

Soak the poppy seeds in the milk overnight. Drain the poppy seeds and pass through a sieve or mash well. Make sure the seeds are dry. Combine the egg yolks, sugar, butter and almonds with the poppy seeds. Add the cornstarch and mix until it is completely dissolved. Slowly fold in the egg whites and cream. Melt the butter into a baking tin and sprinkle with the breadcrumbs. Gently pour in the poppy-seed mixture and bake at 325° for thirty-five to forty minutes until the cakes springs back to the touch.

*

WHITE CAKE
(Slovenia)

4 egg whites, stiffly beaten	½ c. ground walnuts
½ c. sugar	½ c. raisins
½ c. sifted flour	½ c. butter, melted

Chocolate Sauce:

1 c. sugar
½ tsp. vanilla
1 tbsp. butter

½ c. water
1 square chocolate, grated

Beat together the flour, sugar and butter. Slowly fold in the egg whites. Add the raisins and walnuts. Gently pour the batter into a greased and floured baking tin and bake in the oven at 350° for half an hour, or until golden brown. Combine the sugar, water and grated chocolate. Bring to a boil in the top of a double boiler and cook for five minutes, stirring constantly. Remove from heat and allow to cool slightly. Add the butter and vanilla and continue stirring for five minutes. Pour this chocolate sauce over the cake.

*

BUTTERMILK CAKE
(Bulgaria)

2½ c. flour, sifted
2 eggs, well beaten
1¾ c. buttermilk
½ tsp. salt
¾ c. sugar

¾ c. butter
1 tsp. baking powder
1 tbsp. grated lemon rind
½ tsp. baking soda
confectioner's sugar

Cream the butter and sugar together. Add the eggs slowly, beating constantly. Stir in the buttermilk and lemon rind. Sift together the flour, salt, baking soda and baking powder. Add the flour to the eggs and butter, a little at a time, beating after every addition. Pour the batter into a well-greased and floured baking tin and bake in the oven at 350° for 35 minutes. Turn the cake out onto a cooling rack. Cool for five minutes, then sprinkle with powdered sugar.

*

HONEY COOKIES
(Poland)

2¼ c. flour, sifted
2 eggs, well beaten
3 tbsp. milk
½ c. butter
1 c. honey
1 c. ground filberts

½ c. brown sugar
1 tsp. baking soda
2 c. raisins
½ tsp. cinnamon
½ tsp. ginger
½ tsp. nutmeg
½ tsp. salt

Sift the flour, baking soda and salt together. Cream the butter, honey and brown sugar together until smooth. Beat in the eggs and milk. Add the flour, cinnamon, ginger and nutmeg. Beat well. Add the filberts and raisins and mix well. Grease a cookie sheet and drop spoonfuls of batter onto the sheets. Bake the cookies at 400° for ten to fifteen minutes. Makes four dozen cookies.

*

*

BABKA
(Poland)

12 egg yolks	1 tbsp. lemon rind
4 c. flour	1 tbsp. orange rind
1 c. warm milk	2 packages dry yeast
¼ c. warm water	½ c. butter
¾ c. sugar	1 c. raisins
1 tsp. salt	1 c. chopped almonds
1 tsp. vanilla	confectioner's sugar

Dissolve the yeast in the warm water. Add the yeast, salt and milk to half the flour and beat well. Allow the dough to rise until doubled in size. Beat the egg yolks until they become lemon-colored. Add the sugar and beat well. Fold the egg yolks into the dough. Add the remaining flour and work into an elastic dough. Combine the vanilla, the butter, the raisins, the lemon rind, orange rind and the almonds. Mix well and add into the dough. Punch down and continue working the dough until smooth. Place the dough in a greased fluted baking pan. Cover the pan and allow the dough to rise at room temperature for one hour. Bake the Babka in a moderate oven at 350° for one hour. Allow to cool. Combine the confectioner's sugar with warm water to make a sugar glaze. Pour the glaze over the Babka before serving.

*

*

CHOCOLATE MERINGUES
(Czechoslovakia)

4 egg whites
1 c. sugar

2 squares chocolate,
    melted
½ tsp. vanilla

Beat the egg whites until stiff. Add the sugar, a little at a time, and continue beating after each addition. Gently stir in the chocolate and vanilla. Drop spoonfuls of meringue onto a greased cookie sheet. Bake the meringues at 275° for one hour.

*

JAM COOKIES
(The Ukraine)

3 c. flour
2 eggs, lightly beaten
1/4 lb. butter
½ c. raspberry jam

½ c. sour cream
2 cooked egg yolks
2 tbsp. sugar
½ tsp. salt

Sift the flour and place on a board. Make a well in the center and add the eggs, mashed egg yolks, salt, sugar, sour cream and butter. Work the ingredients into a dough. Knead the dough until it is smooth. Cover and allow to sit for an hour. Roll the dough out thinly and cut into squares 3 inches wide.

Dot each square of dough with jam and fold the corners of the squares toward the center. Grease a cookie sheet and bake the cookies at 350° for fifteen minutes.

*

KREMPITA
(Croatia)

Flaky Pastry Dough:

2 c. unsalted butter
4 c. sifted pastry flour
2 tbsp. rum

1 c. ice water
1 tsp. salt

Refrigerate all ingredients and utensils before attempting to make Flaky Pastry Dough. Throughout, the ingredients and utensils must be kept very cold for flaky pastry to be successful. Sift the salt and 3½ cups of flour twice into a deep bowl. Add the rum and ¾ cup of ice water. If necessary, add as much of the remaining water as required to make a stiff paste. The paste should not be too hard, although it must be hard enough to hold the butter. If it is too soft, the butter will be squeezed out. If you can achieve the same consistency of the butter and the paste, then the pastry will roll out very well. Roll the paste out on a floured board thin enough to hold the butter, but not less than ¼". Cut the butter into small chunks. Place one quarter of the butter over the rolled paste. Sift the remaining flour over the butter. Roll the pastry like a jelly roll, then roll it flat with a rolling pin. Place another half cup of butter over the pastry. Roll up again, then flatten with the rolling pin. Continue in this manner until all the butter is used up. Roll the pastry into a rectangle. Fold one third over the center, and the other third over the first. Flatten with the rolling pin. Repeat this three more times, alternating the direction of the fold. Work quickly so that the ingredients remain cool. If necessary, refrigerate several times during the procedure to keep the pastry cold. Refrigerate for at least two hours before baking.

Filling:

8 egg whites	1¼ c. sugar
8 egg yolks	2 c. whipping cream
3 c. milk	½ c. powdered sugar
1 c. flour	1 square semi-sweet
1 vanilla pod	chocolate, grated

Divide the Flaky Pastry Dough into two parts. Roll each section into a rectangle. Place on an ungreased baking sheet and bake in a hot oven at 450° for ten minutes. Reduce the heat to 400° and continue baking until lightly browned on top. Allow to cool. Scald the milk with the vanilla pod. Beat the egg yolks with half the sugar. Add the milk and flour alternately. Bring this mixture to a boil in the top of a double boiler. Cook, stirring constantly, until the mixture thickens. Beat the egg whites until very stiff. Beat the remaining sugar into the stiffly beaten egg whites. Add the egg whites to the egg yolk mixture and continue cooking for another minute. Spread the cream filling over a sheet of cooled flaky pastry. The cream should be no less than 1½" thick. Place another flaky pastry sheet over the filling. Whip the cream. Add the confectioner's sugar. Pipe the whipped cream mixture over the cream filled sheets. Sprinkle with grated chocolate. Dip a very sharp knife in boiling water, then cut the pastry sheets carefully into cream slices. Be sure to cut through the bottom pastry sheet. Sprinkle with confectioner's sugar. The cream slices can be refrigerated before serving.

*

PRUNE KOLACHE
(Czechoslovakia)

½ c. warm milk	2 packages dry yeast
½ c. warm water	¾ c. butter
½ c. sugar	1 tsp. salt
4 egg yolks	4 ½ c. sifted flour

Dissolve the yeast in the warm water. Beat the butter, sugar, salt and egg yolks together. Add the yeast, warm milk and half the flour. Mix well. Slowly add remaining flour and work into a soft dough. Place in a greased bowl; cover and allow to rise until doubled in size. Punch down the dough and turn out onto a floured board. Knead the dough again. Roll the dough out and cut into three-inch circles. Place the circles on greased baking sheets. Allow the dough to double in size. Press a hollow in the center of each and fill with prune filling. Bake at 350° for 15-20 minutes until golden.

Prune Filling:

1½ c. prunes, chopped	2 c. water
2 tbsp. sugar	dash of nutmeg
	2 tsp. orange rind, grated

Combine the ingredients and cook over low heat until a thick syrup forms. Use the filling above as directed.

*

*

CINNAMON COOKIES
(Slovenia)

2 c. sifted flour
2 tsp. cinnamon
1 c. sugar
1 tsp. vanilla

½ c. butter
2 eggs. well beaten
2 tsp. baking powder
¼ tsp. salt

Sift together the flour, salt and baking powder. Cream the butter and sugar. Add the vanilla,cinnamon, and eggs. Beat well. Add the flour and mix well into a thick batter. Grease a cookie sheet and drop spoonfuls of batter onto it. Bake the cookies in the oven at 400° for ten to fifteen minutes. Makes 3 dozen.

*

SOUR CREAM CAKE
(The Ukraine)

⅓ c. flour
6 egg yolks, well beaten
6 egg whites, stiffly beaten

3 c. sour cream
1½ c. sugar
½ tsp. vanilla

Beat the sour cream. Beat the egg yolks until they become frothy and lemon-colored. Add the sugar and beat well. Add the egg yolks to the sour cream. Gently fold in the egg whites and the vanilla. Stir in the flour slowly, being careful not to

---

form lumps. Grease and flour a baking tin and bake the cake in the oven at 350°, for about half an hour until golden brown and the cake springs back to the touch.

*

ALMOND AND HAZELNUT TORTE
(Poland)

¾ c. ground almonds   1¼ c. sugar
¼ c. ground hazelnuts   10 egg whites, stiffly beaten
10 egg yolks   ¼ c. breadcrumbs

Filling:

½ c. strong coffee   1 c. butter
2 egg yolks   ¾ c. powdered sugar

Cream the egg yolks and sugar together. Add the almonds, hazelnuts and breadcrumbs. Mix well. Gently fold in the egg whites. Line three shallow baking tins with greased paper and grease the sides. Pour the batter into the tins. Place the tins in the oven and bake at 325° until golden and springy. For the filling, cream the butter and add the egg yolks, sugar and coffee. Beat the filling well. Remove the torte layers from the oven and allow to cool on a cooling rack. When the layers have cooled completely, spread one layer of the torte with half the filling. Place a second layer on top and cover it with the remaining filling. Place the third layer on top. Make a glaze from confectioner's sugar and warm coffee. Pour the glaze over the torte.

*

*

ZAGREB TORTE
(Croatia)

8 egg yolks
1 c. sugar
1 c. ground almonds

1 c. ground walnuts
3 tbsp. flour
8 egg whites, stiffly beaten

Frosting:

1 c. sugar
5 tbsp. water

2 tbsp. rum
3 egg whites

Beat the egg yolks until they become light and lemon-colored. Add the sugar and continue beating until light and fluffy. Add the nuts and flour and mix lightly. Carefully fold in the stiffly beaten egg whites. Pour into three greased and floured 8" cake pans. Bake at 350° until the torte springs back to the touch. Cook the sugar in the water until it thickens to a medium syrup. Stir in the rum. Stiffly beat the egg whites until they stand in peaks. Add the sugar and beat well. Fold the egg whites into the sugar syrup and beat well. Frost the torte with this mixture. If desired, pour a chocolate glaze over the torte and decorate with walnut halves.

*

*

BOHEMIAN TORTE
(Czechoslovakia)

10 egg whites	1 c. sugar
¾ c. flour	¾ c. ground hazelnuts
2 squares grated chocolate	3½ c. confectioner's sugar
2 c. butter	1 c. cocoa

Beat the egg whites until they stand in peaks. Add the sugar and continue beating until stiff. Add the flour and hazelnuts. Mix well. Grease and flour three 8" cake pans and pour the batter into the pans. Bake at 325° until the torte springs back to the touch. Remove from the oven and allow to cool. Whip the butter and confectioner's sugar together to make a creamy filling. Blend in the cocoa and continue beating until light and fluffy. Frost one layer with chocolate butter cream and top with another layer of torte. Top the second layer with chocolate butter cream. Place the remaining layer of torte on top and frost the tops and sides of the torte with chocolate butter cream. Sprinkle with grated chocolate.

*

WALNUT TORTE
(Poland)

5 egg whites, stiffly beaten	1 tsp. orange rind, grated
3 c. ground walnuts	¾ c. sugar

5 egg yolks
1 c. confectioner's sugar
¼ c. cream

2 tbsp. breadcrumbs
1 tsp. vanilla

Chocolate Frosting:

1 cup butter

1½ c. confectioner's sugar
½ c. cocoa.

Beat the egg yolks until very light and lemon-colored. Add the sugar and continue beating until light and fluffy. Add the orange rind. Fold in the egg whites, half the walnuts and the breadcrumbs. Grease and flour three 8" cake pans and pour in the batter. Bake at 350° for 35 minutes. Combine the confectioner's sugar, vanilla, remaining walnuts and the cream. Mix well. Allow the torte to cool. Spread a layer of torte with half the filling and place a second layer of torte on top. Cover that layer with the remaining filling and place the third torte layer on top. Make a chocolate frosting by whipping together the butter, confectioner's sugar and cocoa until light and creamy. Spread this frosting over the top and sides of the torte.

*

MAKOVNJAČA—POPPY SEED ROLL
(Croatia)

3½ c. flour
¾ c. milk
¼ c. sugar
2 cakes yeast
1 tsp. vanilla

2 egg yolks
1 tsp. lemon rind, grated
6 tbsp. melted butter
½ tsp. salt

Allow the yeast to rise in one quarter cup of warm milk, until doubled in size. Sift the flour into a deep bowl. Make a well in the center and place the yeast in the well. Add the remaining milk, sugar, egg yolks, lemon rind, vanilla, butter and salt. Mix together well and beat with a wooden spoon until blisters begin to form on the dough. Place in a greased bowl, cover with a damp towel and allow to rise in a warm place for about an hour or until doubled in bulk. Divide the dough into two sections. Roll each section out very thin on a floured tablecloth, brush with melted butter and fill with poppy seed filling. Roll the dough by lifting the edge of the tablecloth on which the dough was rolled out. Place the two sections of makovnjaca on a well-greased baking sheet and allow to rise in a warm, draft-free place for another half hour. Brush the rolls with a well beaten egg white and bake at 350° for about an hour until they become golden. Cool before slicing and serving.

Filling:

2 c. ground poppy seeds	4 tbsp. honey
½ c. sweet cream	½ tsp. cinnamon
3 tbsp. raisins	1 tbsp. rum
½ c. sugar	1 tsp. lemon rind

Mix the finely ground poppy seeds, the lemon rind, raisins, sugar and cinnamon. Spread this mixture over the rolled out dough. Heat the cream. Combine the cream, honey and rum and pour this mixture over the poppy seeds. Roll up the dough as described above.

*

*

OREHNJAČA—WALNUT ROLL
(Croatia)

makovnjaca dough
½ c. melted butter
¾ c. sugar
1 c. hot milk
2 tbsp. strawberry jam

1 lb. walnuts, ground
1 tsp. grated lemon peel
¼ c. raisins
1 tsp. cinnamon
2 tbsp. rum

Prepare the orehnjaca *dough in the same manner as the* makonjaca *dough above. Pour the scalded milk over the walnuts. Combine with the remaining ingredients and allow to cool before spreading over the dough. Fill the dough with the walnut filling and bake according to the directions for* makovnjaca.

*

POPPY-SEED LOAF
(The Ukraine)

1 c. poppy seeds, ground
1 c. butter
3 egg yolks, lightly beaten
3 egg whites, stiffly beaten
2 tsp. vanilla

1 c. milk
2 c. sugar
2 c. flour
2 tsp. baking powder
¼ tsp. salt
confectioner's sugar

Soak the poppy seeds in milk for two hours. Cream the butter and sugar together and add the egg yolks and vanilla. Add the poppy seeds and beat well. Sift together the flour, baking powder and salt. Slowly add the flour to the eggs and poppy seeds. Work into a dough. Fold in the egg whites slowly. Grease and flour a narrow baking dish. Pour the dough into the pan and bake at 350° for one hour. Allow to cool slightly, cut in serving portions and sprinkle with confectioner's sugar.

*

TEA COOKIES
(Russia)

1 c. butter	¾ c. almonds, finely
2 c. flour	chopped
1 tsp. vanilla	1 c. powdered sugar
¼ tsp. almond extract	dash of salt

Cream the butter and sugar together until well blended. Add the flour and salt, and then the almonds, vanilla and almond extract. Refrigerate the dough for one or two hours. Break off pieces of dough and place on a greased cookie sheet. Bake the cookies at 400° until golden brown. Sprinkle with powdered sugar and serve with tea. Makes 4 dozen cookies.

*

*

APPLE MAZUREK
(Poland)

2¼ c. ground almonds   2¼ c. flour
1½ c. butter   1½ c. confectioner's sugar
6 egg whites, stiffly beaten   1 tsp. vanilla

Filling:

4 apples, peeled and sliced   ½ tsp. cinnamon
1 c. water   2 c. sugar

Beat the butter until light and fluffy. Add the sugar, vanilla and almonds. Beat the egg whites and flour into the butter mixture, alternately, beating well after each addition. Work into a smooth dough. Roll out to ¼" thickness. Grease and flour a wide and shallow cookie sheet. Place the dough on the sheet and bake at 350° for 20-30 minutes. Place the water, apples, cinnamon and sugar in a pan. Stew the apples over low heat until a thick sauce has formed. Remove the mazurek from the oven when done and allow to cool. Cut the mazurek into two sections. Place the apple sauce over one half of the mazurek and top with the remaining dough. A glaze may be made from confectioner's sugar and water and poured over the mazurek.

*

*

NUT MERINGUES
(Czechoslovakia)

5 egg whites	½ c. ground walnuts
¾ c. water	½ c. ground almonds
2 c. sugar	¼ tsp. salt
¼ tsp. cream of tartar	1 tsp. vanilla

Cook the sugar in the water for about fifteen minutes to make a medium syrup. Beat the egg whites until stiff. Add the salt and cream of tartar. Slowly add the egg whites to the sugar syrup after it has cooled slightly. Add the almonds, walnuts and vanilla. Fill a pastry tube with the meringue and squeeze onto a greased baking dish. Bake at 275° for one hour.

*

POTICA—NUT ROLL
(Slovenia)

½ c. ground filberts	⅓ c. warm milk
½ c. ground walnuts	1 c. butter
2 c. sifted flour	2 egg whites, stiffly beaten
1 package of yeast	4 egg yolks
¼ c. sugar	2 tsp. grated lemon rind
1 tbsp. rum	½ tsp. cinnamon
	½ c. raisins

Pour the rum over the raisins and let them soak for about half an hour. Dissolve the yeast in milk. Slowly add the flour, lemon rind, three egg yolks, ⅓ cup of butter and a ¼ cup of sugar. Work the mixture into a smooth dough. Place the dough in a greased bowl, cover with a towel and allow to rise until doubled in size. Cream the remaining butter and sugar together. Add the last egg yolk, walnuts, filberts, raisins and cinnamon. Stir in the stiffly beaten egg whites. Work into a smooth dough. Roll out the dough until ¼ inch thick; cover with the filling and roll it up. Place the loaf onto a greased baking sheet and allow to rise for one hour. Brush the top of the roll with butter. Bake the potica at 350° for 30-40 minutes.

*

CROATIAN VANILLA COOKIES
(Croatia)

1 c. butter	1 egg yolk
1 whole egg	1 tsp. vanilla
1 egg white, stiffly beaten	½ c. ground nuts
3 c. flour	juice half lemon
	vanilla sugar

Cream the butter until it is light and fluffy. Add the whole egg and the egg yolk and beat until the mixture becomes very creamy. Gradually add the flour, vanilla, nuts and lemon juice. Knead the dough until soft. Roll it out to about one quarter inch thickness. Cut into little circles, crescents, squares and/or diamonds with a cookie cutter. Place on a greased baking sheet. Bake at 350°. Remove from the oven, *and while the cookies are still hot, dip them in the beaten egg white and roll in vanilla sugar.*

*

HONEY AND NUT ROLLS
(Bulgaria)

Dough:

2 eggs
4 c. flour

3 tbsp. oil
1 c. warm water
1/2 tsp. salt

Filling:

2 c. almonds, chopped
¼ c. sugar
1 c. oil

½ tsp. cinnamon
2 tsp. orange rind

Syrup:

2 c. honey
2 c. sugar
1 c. warm water

½ tsp. cream of tartar
juice ½ a lemon

Beat the eggs, salt, oil and warm water together. Add the flour and knead into a smooth dough. If necessary, coat the hands with oil to keep the dough from sticking. Let the dough sit for two to three hours covered with a damp towel to keep from drying out. Divide the dough into six balls. Roll the dough out onto a floured tablecloth and pull the dough with the fingers until the dough is paper thin. Coat a sheet of dough with melted butter, then place a sheet over it. Place a third sheet on top of the second buttered sheet and coat with melted butter. Combine the filling ingredients and place half the filling over the three dough sheets. Roll the dough up tightly and place in a greased baking pan. Place another three sheets of dough on top each other and then the remaining filling on top. Roll up this dough tightly and place next to the first roll in the pan. Slice the rolls into two-inch sections and drizzle lightly with butter. Bake the rolls in the oven at 350° for 45 minutes. Combine the ingredients for the topping and pour immediately over each roll when they are removed from the oven. Allow the rolls to sit at least two to three hours before serving.

*

RUM BABA
(Poland)

4 c. flour	2 tbsp. sugar
1 cake yeast	4 eggs
¼ c. milk	¼ c. raisins
½ c. rum	1 c. sugar
¾ c. water	¼ tsp. salt
¼ c. softened butter	

Warm the milk. Add one tablespoon of sugar and the yeast to the milk. Allow the yeast to rise in the warm milk. Sift the four with the salt twice into a deep bowl. Make a well in the center. Place the yeast in the well. Add the eggs and work into a smooth dough. The dough should be very soft, but *should not stick to the hand or the bowl. Distribute the butter in small pats over the dough. Cover and allow to rise in a warm place until it has doubled in size. Add the remaining tablespoon of sugar to the dough and punch down so that the dough will absorb the butter. Add the raisins and mix very well. Butter one large mold or individual molds and fill each three quarters full. Bake at 400° until the tops are golden brown. Allow to cool completely before turning out of the molds. Cook the water and 1 cup of sugar with the rum until thickened into a syrup. Place the cooked Rum Baba on a wire rack and pour the syrup over them. Allow the cake(s) to drain for eght to ten minutes. If desired, sprinkle with a little more rum. Decorate with whipped cream and fresh fruit before serving.*

*

SPRING TORTE
(Croatia)

1¼ c. sugar	10 eggs
1¼ c. ground walnuts	1 c. chopped dates
1 c. raisins	1 c. chopped figs
rind ½ lemon, grated	4 squares chocolate
1 c. whipped cream	fresh or candied fruit

Beat the egg yolks and the sugar together until the mixture is light and lemon colored. Add the walnuts, dates, raisins, figs and melted chocolate. Stiffly beat the egg whites and fold into the mixture. Pour this batter into a shallow greased and floured cake pan and bake at 325° for about thirty minutes. Allow to cool completely, then garnish with whipped cream piped around the torte and decorate with the fresh or candied fruit.

BREADS

BREADS

*

WHITE BREAD

6 c. sifted flour
1 cake of yeast
1 tsp. salt
2 tbsp. sugar

¼ c. warm water
2 tbsp. shortening
2 c. milk, scalded

Allow the yeast to rise in the warm water to which the sugar has been added for five to ten minutes. Add the salt and shortening to the milk. Add the milk mixture and the yeast to half the flour. Work into a smooth dough adding more flour a little at a time. Place the dough in a greased bowl and allow to double in size, covered with a damp cloth. Punch down the dough and knead again. Separate the dough into two loaves and allow to sit for fifteen minutes. Place the dough into greased pans and allow to rise until it is doubled in size. Bake at 400° for fifteen minutes; then lower the heat to 375° and bake for an additional 35 minutes.

*

RYE BREAD
(Poland)

8 c. rye flour
1 tbsp. sugar

2 c. warm water
2 c. sifted white flour

1 tsp. salt   1 cake of yeast
4 tbsp. caraway seeds

Combine the warm water and half the rye flour and allow to sit in a warm place for two days to ferment. Combine the remaining rye flour, white flour, caraway seeds, fermented flour, sugar, salt and yeast. Work the ingredients into a dough. Place the dough in a greased bowl and allow it to rise until doubled in size. Punch down and make into loaves. Allow the loaves to rise again until doubled in size. Brush with beaten egg whites. Bake at 425° for one hour.

*

POTATO BREAD
(Czechoslovakia)

4 c. sifted flour   2 c. mashed potatoes
1 tbsp. shortening   ½ c. warm water
1 tbsp. sugar   ½ c. boiling water
1½ tsp. salt   1 cake yeast

Combine the yeast, warm water and 1 teaspoon sugar. Allow to stand for ten minutes. Combine the salt, shortening and tablespoon sugar and add to the boiling water. Allow the water to cool to lukewarm and add in the yeast, flour and potatoes. Work into a smooth dough and place in a greased bowl and cover with a cloth. Let it rise until doubled in size. Punch down the dough and let it rise again until doubled in size. Cut the dough in half and shape into loaves. Place in greased loaf tins and bake in the oven at 400° for ten minutes, reduce the temperature to 375° and bake for another 45 minutes.

*

STEAMED WHITE BREAD
(Slovenia)

5 c. flour
½ tbsp. salt
1 cake of yeast

1¼ c. warm milk
½ tbsp. malt extract
1 tbsp. fat

Sift together the salt and the flour. Dissolve the yeast in the milk and allow to rise for about ten minutes. Add the fat and malt extract to the milk. Add the yeast and the milk to the flour. Work into a firm dough. Allow it to sit for half an hour, covered. Punch down the dough and let it rise again. Shape the dough into a loaf and place on a greased baking tin. Place a pan of warm water in the oven and heat the oven to 425°. Place the dough in the oven and bake for five to ten minutes. Remove the warm water and continue baking for 30-45 minutes or until the bread is golden brown.

*

CORNMEAL BREAD
(Bulgaria)

2 cakes of yeast
½ c. warm water
¼ c. butter
1 egg
1 c. corn meal

½ c. sugar
1½ tsp. salt
¾ c. milk, scalded
4 c. flour

Dissolve the yeast in warm water. Cream the butter, sugar and salt. Add the hot milk and mix well. Allow it to cool until warm and add the egg, one cup of flour, the cornmeal and the yeast mixture. Beat the mixture, then slowly add the remaining flour. Work the dough on a floured board until smooth. Place the dough in a greased bowl and allow to rise until doubled in size. Punch down the dough and cut in half. Place the dough on two greased baking sheets and shape into loaves. Cover the dough and allow to rise until doubled in size. Brush with beaten egg white. Bake the bread at 350° for 45 minutes.

*

HARD ROLLS
(Croatia)

8 c. flour	1 tbsp. salt
2 tbsp. melted butter	2 c. milk
2 cakes of yeast	1 tsp. sugar
1 egg white	

Place a pan of water in the oven and preheat to 350°. Scald the milk. Cool to lukewarm. Add the sugar and yeast and allow to rise in a warm place. Sift the flour. Add the butter, salt, and yeast mixture. Mix well to form a firm dough. Knead until very smooth. Allow to rise for half an hour in a warm, draft-free place. Punch down. Allow to sit for ten minutes. Divide the dough into twenty pieces. Shape each piece into a roll and score the tops with short diagonal cuts. Place on a greased baking sheet which has been sprinkled with cornmeal. Sprinkle with poppy seeds or sesame seeds if desired. *Allow to rise for another half hour. Beat the egg white with a little warm water. Brush the rolls with the beaten egg white. Bake at 350° for about half an hour. Remove the pan of water when the rolls have been in the oven for ten minutes.*

*

WHOLE-WHEAT BREAD
(The Ukraine)

5 c. sifted white flour	½ c. sugar
3 c. whole-wheat flour	3 packages dry yeast
2 c. warm water	2 c. warm milk
½ c. warm oil	2 eggs
1 tsp. salt	

Combine the whole wheat flour, sugar, salt and yeast. Add the oil, water and milk. Mix well. Add the eggs to the mixture and beat well. Slowly mix in the white flour to make a stiff dough. Place the dough in a greased bowl and allow to sit, covered, until doubled in size. Punch down the dough and cut in half. Place the dough in greased loaf tins and allow to rise for half an hour. Bake in the oven at 375° for 45 minutes. Before baking, brush the dough with melted butter.

*

*

BLACK BREAD
(Russia)

3 c. rye flour
1 c. white flour
1 tsp. salt
1 package yeast

½ tsp. caraway seeds
2 c. warm milk
1 tbsp. black molasses

Dissolve the yeast in half the warm milk. Add one cup of rye flour and mix well. Allow the yeast and flour to rise until doubled in size. Combine the remaining warm milk with the molasses and salt. Add the milk, caraway seeds, and remaining flour to the yeast. Work into a dough and knead well. Place the dough in a greased bowl and allow to double in size. Punch down. Divide the dough in half and place on greased baking sheets. Brush the dough with butter and bake at 350° for and hour to an hour and a half.

INDEX